BLACK HOLE CHASERS

ANNA CROWLEY REDDING

SQUARE
FISH

FEIWEL AND FRIENDS
New York

SQUARE
FISH

An imprint of Macmillan Publishing Group, LLC
120 Broadway, New York, NY 10271 • mackids.com

Square Fish and the Square Fish logo are trademarks of Macmillan
and are used by Feiwel and Friends under license from Macmillan.

Our books may be purchased in bulk for promotional, educational, or
business use. Please contact your local bookseller or the Macmillan
Corporate and Premium Sales Department at (800) 221-7945 ext. 5442 or
by email at MacmillanSpecialMarkets@macmillan.com.

Library of Congress Control Number: 2020911023

Originally published in the United States by Feiwel and Friends
First Square Fish edition, 2024
Book designed by Raphael Geroni
Square Fish logo designed by Filomena Tuosto
Printed in the United States of America by Lakeside Book Company,
Harrisonburg, Virginia

ISBN 978-1-250-34687-2
1 3 5 7 9 10 8 6 4 2

AR: 6.8 / LEXILE: 920L

To Liam, with love and gratitude,
for keeping my feet on the ground and my
eyes focused on the stars

TABLE of CONTENTS

INTRODUCTION

MONSTERS

A black hole has come for Central City. Chaos erupts. People scramble for cover because, there, in the clear blue sky, is a churning black sphere. Whipping around the black void is a fiery red-orange disk filled with what's left of stars and other cosmic crumbs.

And worse? The black hole's powerful gravity is more than Central City can withstand. Street lamps hurl toward the black void. Skyscrapers fracture and give way. Like an epic super-vacuum cleaner, the black hole is ripping everything apart brick by brick—doom is certain. That's unless comic book superhero the Flash, aka Barry, can save Central City and the planet by flying into that ominous point of no return. Can Barry overcome the most powerful force known to exist?

POP CULTURE ALERT! Emmy award–winning TV series *The Flash* premiered in 2014, telling the story of scientist Barry Allen, who is struck by lightning and gains super speed, becoming the fastest man alive. Like any superhero going about his own business, trouble quickly follows, and Barry (the Flash) must use his power for good! This popular TV show, inspired by the comic book series of the same name, is seven seasons strong and still going (as of this writing). Comic Creator: DC Comics; Run: 1940 through 2016. Tagline: "Lightning fast action, mystery, and adventure."

Too bad Barry can't ask the crew of the Starship *Enterprise* for advice. They know what it's like to stare down a black hole. In the 2009 movie *Star Trek*, they find out the hard way what happens when you fly too close to a black hole. Even at warp speed, there is no escape. Cracks spread across the ceiling of the ship. The black hole appears in flashes and it is breathtaking in size and semi-invisibility. The famous spaceship is helpless against the forces of gravity. The black hole is like a magnet with supernatural control. If they don't come up with a plan, the *Enterprise* and her crew will be lost to the black depths forever.

These plot twists have all the right stuff: clever fiction, actual science—all tossed together for an outrageous adventure. And let's face it, there is no other cosmic character that commands such credible and certain destruction as a black hole! Powerful. Deadly. Unseen. Nothing in space captures our imaginations like black holes. Nothing.

Black holes are a reliable "go-to" when it comes to drumming up drama, ratcheting up tension, summoning suspense, and hinting at locked secrets of the universe and those inside ourselves.

After all, black holes gobble up anything that gets too close. That much we know. But beyond the basics, black holes represent the limits of human knowledge itself!

Yes, black holes can be the perfect partner in our efforts to explain what we long to discover. *Are black holes portals to another universe? A secret door to an intergalactic highway? Do they stalk galaxies, swallowing stars and planets? Are they capable of scarfing down entire solar systems in one fiery gulp? And what happens if a person is sucked up by a black hole? Will they become a long string of human spaghetti? Are black holes star shredders?* Terrifying *and* fascinating. And that's exactly what makes them so cool!

> **BOOKSHELF:** *The Care and Feeding of a Pet Black Hole* by Michelle Cuevas. The fact that we know so little about black holes makes them the perfect world-building buddy to invent details, powers, and behaviors, like a habit of following kids home from NASA. That's what happens to fictional character Stella Rodriguez. When she visits NASA and a black hole follows her home, she makes a lot of discoveries. She can explain the anatomy of a black hole and she observes how it eats everything in sight. But the one thing it doesn't seem capable of consuming? Her broken heart. This middle-grade book is less of an intense high stakes sci-fi adventure and more of a love letter to black holes and surviving grief.

It's easy to think you know what black holes actually look like. Our imaginations are *that* good. Plus, artists have used every tool they have, from pens and paint to sophisticated computer graphics, to create jaw-dropping images. Like magicians, they made real what we could only imagine. They offered space fans an educated guess, often based on the best science. But even though these images were smart guesses, fancy guesses, visually stunning guesses, they were still—just guesses. These realistic images of a dark force, illuminated only by a bright ribbon of star leftovers slung around this deadly nothingness, well . . . they are so realistic, so awe-inspiring, it's no wonder they make for mind-blowing TV and movie scenes, magazine and book illustrations.

But the truth is that no one had seen a black hole. No one. No human being, no telescope, no space bound probe had ever seen a black hole. Ever.

A scientist named Sheperd Doeleman was determined to change that.

It was an impossible goal. One that promised heart-crushing failure.

The technology they needed did not exist—unless they invented it.

And he couldn't do it alone. He would need a team of scientists to help. But, just like it often happens in comic books, when heroes try to do something impossible, the world was in trouble. Wars were breaking out. Countries were closing their borders. Instead of banding together to solve problems, people were looking at each other with suspicion and distrust.

The quest required nothing less than quick thinking, innovation, perseverance, teamwork, and united dedication to an epic goal: explore and expand the very limits of human knowledge by taking a picture of something that had never been seen before—a black hole.

1

WAIT, WHAT IS A BLACK HOLE IRL?

Black holes are what happens after particularly large stars die. Star death is fairly dramatic—especially when it comes to massive stars, the biggest stars of all. When it's their time to die, massive stars go out in a blaze of glory.

Huge, bright, and superheavy, they must be more than eight times the mass of the Sun to be officially labeled "*massive*." These stars spend their lives growing. Expanding and expanding, fueled by constant nuclear fusions at their core. Gravity pulls the mass of a star to its center. But there is another force pushing the star outward from the center. That's the heat and pressure from the nuclear fuel at the core. These two forces keep a star in check. One pushing out. One pulling in.

That is, until it runs out of fuel.

Then, that multimillion-year-long growth spurt comes to an end and the star collapses in on itself. Imagine those outer edges of the star slamming into the core in less than a second. The impact sets off an enormous explosion. Shock waves rush out into the cosmos. In fact, the explosion is so powerful and large, it has its own name: supernova.

The supernova remnant Cassiopeia is the glowing debris field left behind after a massive star exploded. (Credit: NASA)

LINGO ALERT! Gravitational Collapse. Ugh, let me go! The star's gas is superheated and this creates pressure. And that pressure wants to expand and escape. But ugh, gravity! Gravity just can't let it go. Gravity keeps the star pulled together. And gravitational collapse happens when something contracts or pulls in on itself toward its own center of gravity *because* its own gravity becomes stronger than other forces. In the case of a dying star, gravitational force becomes stronger than the force of pressure from the hot core, because it's run out of fuel. That leads to the star's gravitational collapse.

The post-supernova leftovers collapse once again, shrinking down, down, down into a single point. This teeny tiny point is even smaller than a single atom! It is infinitely small (as in never-ending in its smallness) and it has infinite mass. So, it's pretty heavy. And like any heavy, massive thing, it has powerful gravity. The more mass, the more gravity. Endless amount of mass? Well, that puts its gravity in a whole new category!

ALTERNATIVE MASSIVE STAR AFTERLIVES: Post-supernova, massive star remains can regroup and become a neutron star (superdense and small, neutron stars are full of busy neutrons), or the bits and pieces and dust clouds of former greatness can drift off into outer space.

To get even an inkling of what this is like . . . imagine taking an Egyptian pyramid that weighs nearly six million tons. Now, imagine shrinking it and squishing it until that pyramid is small enough to fit into the palm of your hand—only it still weighs six million tons! But what if that superheavy pocket-size pyramid gobbled up anything that traveled too close to it? And that six million tons of mass keeps growing, becoming heavier and heavier?

That's similar to what happens when a massive star collapses in on itself. Those super squished star leftovers compact down into a single point. That single point is called the singularity.

And the singularity is what scientists believe lies inside black holes.

> Just like stars come in different sizes, so do black holes. Stellar mass black holes are on the smaller side; intermediate black holes make up the middle. And supermassive black holes are the biggest of all. After all, they have at least one MILLION times more mass than our Sun. How these ginormous monsters are born is still a bit of a mystery. Some scientists think they are formed when black holes merge (which sounds friendly and mature, but probably is super violent and awe-inspiring as far as space dramas go).

And even though it's just a teeny tiny point, all of that matter, that mass, has an unbelievably powerful gravitational pull. It is so intense that if anything gets too close, it can't escape. Not even light. The black hole can even bend space itself.

TRAMPOLINE TIME!

||||||||||||||||||||||||||||||||||||||||||||||||||||||||||||||||||||||||||||||||||||||||||||||||||

It's easy to think of space as an endless black nothingness, with stars artfully placed here and there. But as super smart physicist Albert Einstein explained, space is more like fabric. He called this fabric space-time, based on the idea that space and time are connected like different threads that are woven together to create a single fabric. Think about it this way. Right now, you are reading this book . . . at a particular time *and* at a particular location in space. Those two things are connected. He also realized that space-time controls how everything moves in the universe. If there is a bend in space-time, that bend actually changes the way objects move. And what creates changes in space-time? Objects with mass such as you, me, Earth, other planets, and especially black holes.

ALBERT EINSTEIN lived from 1879 to 1955. He was one of the most important scientists of the 20th century. This Nobel Prize–winning physicist is famous for $E=mc^2$. This equation explains the relationship between mass and energy. His theory of general relativity (and more) is still being used and tested today!

Albert Einstein, 1879–1955. (Photo by Orren Jack Turner, via Library of Congress)

Finding this difficult to wrap your head around? Einstein gave us a great example to help us visualize his idea. Imagine the space-time fabric is like the surface of a trampoline. When you roll a bowling ball onto that black rubbery surface, what happens? The trampoline sags. Now imagine you roll golf balls across the trampoline. What will happen to their paths? They will roll toward the bowling ball in a spiral along the curved, sagging surface of the trampoline. The same is true of how things move around a black hole. A black hole's bend in space-time changes the trajectory and orbit of nearby objects. The scientific word for this is the geodetic effect.

LINGO ALERT! Theoretical physicists use physics to explain our world and make predictions about our world. These predictions become theories and those theories are then tested.

EUREKA!
A DAYDREAM THAT
CHANGES THE WORLD

||||||||||||||||||||||||||||||||||||||||||||||||||||||||||||||||||||||||||||||||||||||||||||||||||||

In the early 1900s, everyone accepted Isaac Newton's idea that a mysterious force known as gravity kept planets in place. But when Einstein began thinking about how mass moves through space and time, he realized this idea had its limits.

Einstein conducted a series of *thought experiments* about it—focused daydreams where he used his imagination to think through different problems and scenarios. These thought experiments allowed Einstein to test ideas in his mind's eye, like a virtual laboratory.

Even while working as a clerk in a Swiss patent office, Einstein spent every available minute thinking about the universe and trying to unlock its mysteries. One day he spotted a window washer high on a ladder, scrubbing away. Einstein wondered what they would each experience if the man fell? From Einstein's point of view, the man would appear to be falling fast, straight to the ground. But to the window cleaner, what would *he* experience? Would it seem to him like time had slowed down? Yes! Also, the man would experience weightlessness, because the ground wasn't pushing up against him. This idea gave birth to his theory of special relativity. But his journey to better understand gravity and our cosmos was not over.

Soon, Einstein realized that space-time itself can bend and curve. And if that's true, well then objects must travel along the curved path. He realized that light wasn't merely a wave, but made up of small packets called photons. And that a beam of light, or stream of photons, would also bend as it travels the curve.

During an eclipse of the Sun in 1919, when the Moon blocked almost all of the Sun's light from Earth, it turned day into night. This darkness allowed astronomers to see a star shining right next to the Sun. But astronomers already knew about this star. And actually, it was located *behind* the Sun. It really shouldn't have been visible at all. EXCEPT if you apply Einstein's theory about space-time and light traveling this curve, then we can understand that the star had not moved. Rather, its light was traveling around the Sun's distortion of space-time to reach Earth!

So, Isaac Newton was right. Earth's gravity does affect the Moon, but Einstein figured out how: Earth's mass bends space-time, giving the Moon a path to move around the Earth. Then he wrote down his theory in a set of *field equations*—math problems that would describe the physical field of space-time.

American physicist John Wheeler would later summarize it like this: "Space-time tells matter how to move. Matter tells space-time how to curve."

EINSTEIN'S FIELD EQUATION

$$R_{\mu\nu} - \frac{1}{2} R\, g_{\mu\nu} + \Lambda\, g_{\mu\nu} = \frac{8\pi G}{c^4}\, T_{\mu\nu}$$

(tells matter/energy how to curve space-time)

(tells matter/energy how to move through curved space-time)

But coming up with the equations didn't necessarily mean solving them! Other scientists picked up the torch.

> **PUTTING EINSTEIN TO THE TEST!** Mercury has a wonky, wobbly orbital path. Before Einstein's theories and field equations came along, all scientists had was Newton's theory on universal gravity. And Newton's math failed to predict the path Mercury took around the Sun (which seemed to be constantly changing). Could Einstein's theory do the trick? The answer is yes. Einstein's theory correctly predicted Mercury's orbital path.

In 1916, physicist Karl Schwarzschild examined Einstein's theory of general relativity while thinking about the universe. Looking at the math, Schwarzschild realized the theory of general relativity predicted the existence of a region of space from which nothing could escape. Describing it as a hole in the very fabric of space-time, he believed this hole was shaped like a sphere and that once anything got too close or passed a point of no return, it could not escape.

Thought of another way, it's as if you go into the school bathroom, flush the toilet, and it opens up a dark bottomless pit—one that is capable of swallowing you and everything in the school, town, country, and planet, followed by the universe (sorry if this has been your fear all along) with a single flush.

> **BRAIN BENDER!** Schwarzschild also realized that everything we understand about physics disappears into the black hole because not even information can make its way out.

But when Schwarzschild talked about this wonky region of space that sucked in anything that got too close, well—his idea was met with more of a "meh," than a "wow." Because honestly, what could make a region of space do something like that? No one could figure it out.

Then, in 1935, an astrophysicist named Subrahmanyan Chandrasekhar pulled it together. He was investigating star death. That's when he realized that the gravitational collapse of a star would cause space-time to collapse in on itself. Boom. The whole idea went from a confusing piece of math to astronomical theory.

Still, scientists at that time believed these singularities were extremely rare.

SUBRAHMANYAN CHANDRASEKHAR, Born: 1910 Lahore, Pakistan. Died: August 21, 1995 Chicago, IL. Chandrasekhar was an Indian American astrophysicist who won the Nobel Prize for Physics in 1983 for his discoveries about black holes and massive stars.

Portrait of a young Subrahmanyan Chandrasekhar as Fellow of Trinity College, Cambridge. (Credit: AIP Emilio Segrè Visual Archives, gift of Subrahmanyan Chandrasekhar)

That's until theoretical physicist Stephen Hawking came along! He, along with Roger Penrose, realized that this gravitational collapse was part of a massive star's life cycle.

Just a few years later, John Wheeler was describing this star-death-black-hole-birth idea at a conference and that's when he blurted out a new name for this strange region of space: a black hole!

THE PROOF IS IN
THE PICTURE

Still, it was far from proven.

It's not that no evidence existed. The evidence was strong. Astrophysicists observed the behavior of light and matter orbiting an invisible gravitational behemoth. They could observe stars moving near black holes. Scientists had seen jets of radiation and particles shoot out from black holes. They were not small burps either. These jets can span a distance of 5,000 light-years! So, in 2019, scientists had evidence of black holes. But even with all of that—never, ever had anyone actually *seen* a black hole.

> **LIGHT-YEAR.** Ever wonder just how far light can travel in one Earth year? The answer is roughly 6 trillion miles or 9 trillion kilometers. In numerical form, that's 6,000,000,000,000 miles a year. So, when people refer to an object being one light-year away, now you know they mean 6 trillion miles away. To get to the center of the Milky Way galaxy, you'll need to travel 26,000 light-years!

It's kind of like not knowing for sure that a football game is taking place on a Friday night under the lights. You hear the crowd. You see traffic is heavy near the high school. You can spot a glow in the distance over a sports field. But still, you haven't seen the game for yourself. (Note: In this imaginary world smartphones don't exist and no one texted you a picture.)

So here was the score. Math that predicted black holes? Yes. Evidence of black holes? Yes. But directly observing one and showing that image to the world? No. Big fat zero.

After all, as the saying goes, seeing is believing. A photo would be visual proof of a black hole's existence. It would be the ultimate test of Einstein's theory. An image could show us if any of the evidence, any of the math, was wrong. It would open up a whole new way to study black holes.

But how could you take a picture of a dark spot in space? Like a relay race, the baton for black hole discovery had been passed from Einstein to Schwarzschild to Chandrasekhar to Stephen Hawking. What leap in discovery would come next and who could get the kind of proof that can't be denied . . . a picture? Who would take the baton?

The Anatomy of a Black Hole

EVENT HORIZON: This is the edge of the black hole where matter falls in but cannot escape. Not even light. It is the point of no return. Once you cross the event horizon, you can never leave!

ACCRETION DISK: This disk, like a puffy doughnut, is made up of gas and dust. It swirls around the black hole at nearly light speed, creating some of the most extreme conditions in the known universe. The temperature? Hundreds of billions of degrees! The accretion disk's extreme speeds and friction create electromagnetic radiation. Extreme friction. Extreme radiation.

RELATIVISTIC JET: As a black hole eats matter like stars, dust, or gas, it shoots out some of that material from the accretion disk in jets that travel up to thousands of light-years away!

PHOTON SPHERE: The photon sphere is that bright area around the black hole, just outside the event horizon. Light is being bent around the black hole by its powerful force of gravity. This photon sphere allows us to see the unseeable, that dark shadow in the center, which is the black hole itself.

SINGULARITY: The center of the black hole. This is where matter collapses to a single point of extreme density.

SCHWARZSCHILD RADIUS: Named for the man who solved one of Einstein's most important equations, this term refers to how small of a sphere that matter has to be squished into for it to experience gravitational collapse. Cool fact! For Earth, its Schwarzschild radius would be about the size of a Ping-Pong ball. At that size, it would become a black hole!

SPAGHETTIFICATION: This is a theory about what happens when you get sucked into a black hole. You are pulled in and that enormous force of gravity turns you into a piece of human spaghetti. Luckily, it's a quick process!

TEMPERATURE: Inside a black hole it's unimaginably cold. But on the outside, that's another story. All of that matter hurled around the black hole at close to the speed of light creates intense heat.

This artist's impression depicts a rapidly spinning supermassive black hole surrounded by an accretion disk. This thin disk of rotating material consists of the leftovers of a Sun-like star, which was ripped apart by the tidal forces of the black hole. The black hole is labeled, showing the anatomy of this fascinating object. (Credit: ESO)

CHAPTER 2

CHASING LIGHT
AND SHADOWS

Something exciting was happening. The whole country was turning its attention to space. Stories in magazines, newspapers, and on TV ramped up excitement for weeks. It was all leading up to a big astronomical event—a solar eclipse. The Moon was going to move between the Earth and the Sun, blocking the Sun's light. And the shadow of the eclipse would fall across the northwestern corner of the United States.

As the moments until the eclipse ticked down, news cameras from Oregon to Washington and Montana pointed up to the sky. In New York City, network news anchors sat at their desks explaining to a LIVE national TV audience what was about to happen. Totality. When the Moon traveled in front of the Sun and was dead center— daytime would turn to night!

On February 26, 1979, children sat glued to the television for a chance to see it. But, the lucky people who were physically in the shadow's path were in for a treat. A spectacular view . . . if the weather cooperated.

Twelve-year-old Sheperd Doeleman didn't need any explanation. On that February morning just before 10:00 a.m. (PST), Shep was already at an observatory in Goldendale, Washington (aka ground zero for eclipse watching). Not only was Shep going to witness the event firsthand, but if he had a question, his dad just happened to be a high school science teacher.

> **SET YOUR ALARM CLOCK!** The next solar eclipse to have North America in its path will be on October 14, 2023.

"My mom and dad and I drove to the desert," Shep explained. After a three-hour drive from their home in Portland, Oregon, Shep and his parents took their place in a crowd of thousands of people who wanted to see the eclipse in person. In the excitement, some were chanting, while others beat drums. Chin stretched toward the sky, Shep looked up to witness the big astronomical show.

"And we got ready to see this eclipse," he remembered, "and there were clouds."[1] Clouds. A thick blanket of clouds as far as the eye could see. Totality was coming. Just minutes away. And they could see . . . nothing.

And then, all of sudden, as if by magic . . . the clouds disappeared. The drumming stopped. The crowd fell silent. Shep held up a protective piece of Mylar in front of his face—which allowed him to safely look directly at the eclipse.

A total solar eclipse on Monday, August 21, 2017, above Madras, Oregon. (Credit: NASA/Aubrey Gemignani)

"We got a very wonderful view of the eclipse and that was a very special moment," Shep explained. "You really, really feel small, when you realize that cosmic objects are aligning in just the right way to let you see something that is normally invisible to us: the corona of the sun."[2]

More than forty years later, he can still recall it in vivid detail because that moment grabbed him. Seeing the unseeable. Observing the unknowable. Impossible weather conditions, completely out of our control, and yet, when the Moon blocked out most of the Sun, he could see the outer ring of the Sun, fiery plumes erupting out from our star. He could see and understand something about our cosmos that had been completely hidden just seconds before. He was fascinated. To be clear, it wasn't an obsession with astronomy. As a kid, when the Sun sank below the horizon, he was not glued to a telescope. "You know, I wasn't grinding my own lenses when I was a kid,"[3] Shep said. It was the discovery. He had spent his childhood busting open lava rocks to find hidden crystals inside.

Shep, age thirteen, working at the Oregon Museum of Science and Industry. (Photo courtesy of Sheperd Doeleman)

Now his curiosity was exploding. Shep spent the next seven years racing through school. He entered high school at age twelve, entered college at fifteen, and graduated from college at nineteen years old. This kid who started reading at three years old, who was quick to complain when school wasn't hard enough . . . well, he was on a collision course with a black hole and he didn't even know it.

THE BOTTOM OF THE WORLD

||||||||||||||||||||||||||||||||||||||||||||||||||||||||||||||||||||||||||||||||||||||||||||||||||

Antarctica, McMurdo Station, 1986

Click. Click. Click. The southern lights whipped across the black night sky. Shades of gray and pink fanned out like ribbons and flowing curtains. Shep grabbed his camera. One shot after another. Easy, right? But getting those shots was anything but easy. It wasn't like Shep was taking pics from a comfy backyard, or local mountaintop. No, he was standing in one of the harshest environments on Earth—Antarctica.

Shep should have been at Massachusetts Institute of Technology (MIT).

> **ANTARCTICA:** As the southernmost continent on Earth, Antarctica's 5,500,000 square miles are almost all ice covered. Antarctica has just two seasons: winter and summer. The sun sets in March and won't rise again until September. That's six months of sun twenty-four hours a day and six months of darkness twenty-four hours a day. Winter temperatures at the South Pole can drop as low as 100 degrees below zero Farenheit (-73 degrees Celsius).

After a science-soaked childhood and a light speed education, Shep had been accepted to one of the best universities in the world to get his PhD in physics. As one of the world's most prestigious graduate programs, MIT was impossibly difficult to get into. A degree from MIT would have opened so many doors and paved the way forward. So, Shep *should* have been in Cambridge, Massachusetts. But, in reality, he was just about as far from MIT as anybody possibly could be.

> **MASSACHUSETTS INSTITUTE OF TECHNOLOGY**, aka MIT, was founded in 1861. Motto: "Mens et Manus," which means mind and hand. Location: Cambridge, Massachusetts. Alumni include 95 Nobel laureates. Located across the Charles River from Boston, MA.

During his last days as an undergraduate at Reed College, Shep had passed by a bulletin board that was full of notices for students. One stood out: a job offer for a research position conducting space-based experiments. Oh, and the job was located on the coldest place on Earth: Antarctica. How could he refuse?

It meant walking away from MIT. It required getting to New Zealand, then Antarctica. It meant bracing for a sunless winter with no escape from McMurdo Station, unless, of course, you had an absolutely dire life-and-death problem that would require the US government to evacuate you under very dangerous circumstances. Antarctica is staffed with scientists and support staff throughout the winter. But everyone who chooses to "overwinter" in Antarctica knows the deal: If you want to leave, if you truly want to go home, you must leave before winter. There won't be new staff or new supplies until late spring. That's just how it works. And it takes a certain type of person to be able to take it. No Sun. No new people. Unbelievable cold. No hardware store down the road. It required a "if it breaks you must fix it" kind of person. And Shep was that guy. At nineteen years old, he was the youngest person to spend the winter in Antarctica.

Shep in Shackelton's Hut, Antarctica, 1986.
(Photo courtesy of Sheperd Doeleman)

McMURDO STATION: Antarctica is a hub of scientific research. About 1,000 scientists are there in the winter, and that number can swell up to 5,000 in the summer. Many countries have labs there. Research labs are sprinkled around the continent. The American lab is called McMurdo Station. McMurdo is built on volcanic rock on Antarctica's Ross Island. The station gets its name from Vice Admiral Archibald McMurdo, who was a British naval officer and Antarctic explorer in the early 1800s. Today they have a webcam livestreaming on the National Science Foundation's website!

When Shep first arrived during the Antarctic summer, the Sun was always up, drawing a circle around the sky, yet never setting. But eventually winter came. The Sun disappeared for its months-long retreat, leaving the continent of Antarctica cloaked

Aurora above Shep's lab at McMurdo Station, Antarctica, 1987.
(Photo courtesy of Sheperd Doeleman)

in darkness like nowhere else. It was so cold that if you threw boiling-hot water out the window, it would vaporize instantly.

And there was Shep, frozen planet beneath his feet and an absolute marvel overhead. The night sky. In the rest of the world, light pollution blots out most of the stars in the sky, but in Antarctica, there is not much more than ice, a few warmly dressed humans, and the stars.

Staring up into the Antarctic night sky was like staring into space. For Shep, it was nothing short of amazing. "The best sky I've ever seen in my life. You know, in the middle of nowhere in the bottom of the world, looking up. And that was, that was incredible,"[4] he said. It was like going from watching TV on a static-filled black-and-white television set from the 1960s to putting on a VR headset. The space between you and what you're looking at? Gone.

It focused Shep's perspective on life, science, and what actually excited him about both. Just like when he was a little boy, there was something about finally observing something for the first time . . . something that had been there all along, just out of view. And there was another ingredient forming Shep's future: tinkering, working with all things mechanical to carry out a task, to help answer a question. Conducting science on Antarctica required a practical, hands-on, fix-it sensibility. It was not working eight hours a day in a lab taking notes. It was adventurous. That sense of adventure paired with the need to force the cosmos to reveal secrets . . . that would come in super handy in turning the world's largest telescopes toward a black hole sixty-five million miles away.

DR. SHEPERD DOELEMAN, Astrophysicist

BORN: 1967, Leuven, Belgium

EDUCATION: Reed College, Massachusetts Institute of Technology (MIT)

CHILDHOOD HOBBIES: Building homemade rockets, rock hunting, reading

Sheperd Doeleman building circuits at Maunakea, Hawaii, in 2009.
(Photo courtesy of Sheperd Doeleman)

BOOKSHELF: *The Dragon's Egg* by Robert L. Forward. This 1980 science fiction book captured Shep's attention. The plot centers around life on a neutron star!

Radio Telescopes and How to See an Invisible Sky

Ever see someone use a dog whistle to call a dog? They put the metal whistle to their mouths and blow. We humans can't hear the sound it makes. But dogs, on the other hand, hear it loud and clear and come running!

Try thinking about light in the same way. The light we see with our human eyes is a form of electromagnetic radiation. And we humans only see a small bit of the electromagnetic spectrum. Our sliver is known as visible light.

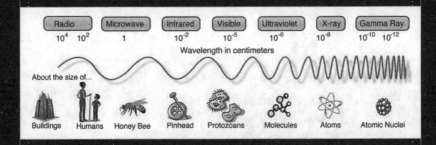

This diagram shows the types of wavelengths in the electromagnetic spectrum going from longest to shortest. (Credit: NASA)

That means when you look up at the night sky, you are only seeing a small part of the picture. Even with powerful optical telescopes, you are still only seeing visible light. That means there is an entire invisible cosmos to explore.

Planets, moons, stars, comets, asteroids, and almost every other cosmic object interact with light. They can emit light themselves. They can reflect light from another source. They can absorb light and transmit light.

When you look at the illustration, you can see that the electromagnetic spectrum is measured by wavelengths. On the long wave range of the electromagnetic spectrum are radio waves, which many objects in space emit. Events like supernovas send out radio light waves, and scientists have even discovered radio waves from the Big Bang!

These signals travel all the way to Earth. But remember, radio waves aren't in the visible light spectrum, so how can we capture them? Radio telescopes!

Scientists use radio telescopes to collect radio light waves, focus and amplify them, and then download that information to powerful computers that sort and compile the data. Then, researchers, astronomers, and scientists use the data to make sense of what the telescope is observing.

NASA suggests thinking of it like this: When you are riding along in your car and want to listen to music on the radio, you tune into the right frequency or channel. Your car's antenna captures these waves. Then, the radio player transforms them into sound waves you can hear.

The night sky as seen through a radio telescope reveals distant galaxies, radiation around black holes, and leftovers from supernova explosions, among many other exciting types of objects to observe. They also provide additional information about objects we see through optical telescopes all the time.

Anna Ho, a radio astronomer, gave the example of looking at the Messier 81 group of galaxies through an optical telescope. Visible light shows you that they are in the same cosmic neighborhood. You can see their shape and learn something about their size. But the same view with a radio telescope shows you that these galaxies actually interact with one another. It looks almost as if currents are swirling in and out of them.

M81/M82/NGC3077   VLA HI mosaic

Yun et al. Nature 1994, 372, 530

Visible light (left) and radio wave (right) image of the galaxies Messier 81, Messier 82, and NGC3077, the main members of the Messier 81 group of galaxies. (Credit: SKA Telescope Archives)

And if scientists want to study these galaxies and currents at super high resolution with a lot of detail, they use an array of radio telescopes. Multiple radio antennae are placed in a group and pointed at the same object at the same time to make observations together. This makes it possible for radio astronomers to combine observations from each antenna. And that correlation process makes the radio telescope larger and more powerful, offering scientists a sharper tool to investigate cosmic bodies. This is called interferometry.

3

PICKING UP THE SCENT

After his year at the bottom of the planet and another year of traveling to other outposts around the world . . . Shep resubmitted an application to MIT. And was accepted a *second* time. One of the cool things about MIT was that they owned an incredible observatory! That meant Shep could work there!

MIT's Haystack Observatory sits atop one of the rolling hills outside Boston, Massachusetts. Drive up the hill, through thick woods on either side, and a huge geodesic dome appears in the clearing at the top. The kind of work done at Haystack, the type of equipment (enormous telescopes) they use, requires not only an understanding of the science involved, but an understanding of the machinery itself, an ability to work on these machines and to travel to far-flung parts of the world when required.

Want to know who was perfect for this? Shep.

LINGO ALERT! Radio Astronomy is a field of science where researchers can not only use radio telescopes to receive light waves from space, but they can also emit them, bouncing radio waves off planets and other cosmic objects to learn more about them, like size, shape, characteristics, and other cool information!

With his MacGyver sensibilities, he was not only at home understanding and exploring the cosmos, but also tinkering with the machinery that was making it possible. Oh, and he knew something about traveling to remote, challenging locations.

TV SHOW: *MacGyver*

YEARS: 1985–1992, 2016 Reboot

PLOT: This fast-paced action adventure TV show centered around the thrilling life of secret agent Angus MacGyver. MacGyver had a habit of finding himself in impossible life-or-death situations. And just as all hope seemed lost, as time ran down to the last second . . . he would use brainpower to fashion whatever objects he could get his hands on (a stick of gum, a paperclip, his trusty Swiss Army knife, or any other ordinary item) into a day-saving solution, just in the nick of time. The series was such a hit that *MacGyvering* quickly became a pop culture verb. Comedy show *Saturday Night Live* even had a regular segment that parodied MacGyver called "MacGruber"!

Shep quickly learned the ropes: how to run the equipment, how to interpret the data, how to work the wall of computers that took up an entire room. He understood the observatory's observational power and the observatory's computing power.

Haystack Observatory. (Credit: Daderot)

HAYSTACK OBSERVATORY

BUILT: 1964 by the US government. Six years later, Haystack became a civilian radio observatory.

LOCATION: Westford, MA

EQUIPMENT: 37-meter Radio Telescope, 18.3-meter Radio Telescope, Radar, and multiple large Radio Antennae, plus a Supercomputer to process the data.

MISSION: To study the structure of the galaxy and universe, to advance the scientific knowledge of our planet and its atmosphere, to enhance technology development to serve radio science and radar sensing, and to contribute to the education and training of the next generation of scientists and engineers.

COOL HISTORY FACT: Back when the US was in a nail-biting space race with Russia—a space race it was losing—NASA needed to determine where to land on the Moon. Haystack was tasked with the job. Using radar, scientists scanned the surface of the Moon. They mapped out craters, smooth plains, and steep mountains, until they found the perfect spot of lunar crust to make history.

Suddenly, Shep, the boy who never fit in as a kid because he had always been too smart, too young, or too "different" after spending part of his childhood in Europe . . . suddenly the outsider was at home and could turn "not fitting in" into a superpower.

He focused on something called Very Long Baseline Interferometry (VLBI). It's a long word and awkward acronym for a simple concept. Remember how an array of telescopes works? They are grouped together on top of a mountain and point at the same object in the sky. VLBI works similarly, but instead of grouping telescopes on the same spot, it links telescopes that are pretty far apart. The distance between the telescopes is called the baseline. A very long baseline means a great distance apart.

> **VLBI:** Very Long Baseline Interferometry. Imagine that you are at a football game with a friend. You both have cameras and start snapping pictures of the field from opposite ends at exactly the same time. Now, imagine you and your friend take those photos and compare them, stitch them together, use any overlap to create even deeper and more richly detailed images. VLBI works in a similar way. You connect two or more telescopes and together they act as one. Like a jigsaw puzzle, each telescope pair offers more detail, more clues, and more information about the cosmic object you are studying.

When you head outside to gaze at the Moon, it can look small in the night sky from where you are standing on Earth—no bigger than your outstretched hand. But when you look at it through a telescope, the image is magnified. Not only does the Moon fill your view, but you can often even see detail on the Moon's surface like craters and ridges. But if you use that same telescope to look at Mars, your view doesn't improve much. You'll need a bigger, more powerful telescope. That's because Mars is so far away.

If you want to see something in space that is very, very far away, like millions and millions and millions of light-years away, you'll need a pretty big telescope. The smaller the object appears from your standpoint, the bigger the telescope you need to see it. The size of the telescope is equally critical in collecting radio waves. And with VLBI, you could build truly gigantic telescopes.

This technology had another exciting promise. Looking once again at the electromagnetic spectrum (which shows the spectrum of light organized by wavelength), you could use VLBI to see the light with the highest frequency or shortest wavelength, called the submillimeter group. And the resolution would be much sharper. When you look through a microscope in science class, at first your view of the slide might be fuzzy, but as you focus it, the resolution becomes sharper and sharper. Submillimeter waves received by giant telescopes offered sharper resolution. And that meant more detail, the best view technology had to offer.

Why was that important or even interesting?

Because it meant an opportunity to see things in the cosmos that were invisible to our human eyes and that even our telescopes had not yet been able to "see." Remember, our human eyes are just limited to seeing *visible* light. So every time we look at the universe with a new tool, we see things we never could before. It's a chance to make new discoveries, which can lead to scientific breakthroughs. And that means explaining parts of our universe that are not well understood. If successful, this innovation could even be used to study one of the cosmos's best kept secrets—black holes.

Other radio waves could not get past all the space dust and debris between Earth and Sagittarius A*. Think about looking out your window trying to see what the dog is doing in the backyard. If your window is dusty and translucent, you can't quite see what the dog is doing, though maybe the movement of her shape could give you a clue. But you'll need a transparent glass window to actually *see* what she's up to.

Using VLBI to observe those high-frequency submillimeter waves of light offered a potential way to see right through all of that galactic blur and murky matter!

The team at Haystack was aggressively working on this, as were astronomers around the world. Each small success, each bit of progress was published. Other astronomers could read about the new developments and incorporate that knowledge into their own efforts.

Not only did the work require computer code, algorithms, and observation time, it also required traveling to radio telescopes around the world and adjusting them to look at the same point in space at the same time. And these radio telescopes were originally built to collect lower-frequency light, not submillimeter. So, adjustments had to be made and they had to be made in person, tools in hand.

The road ahead would be years long and would carry Shep through his graduation and beyond. But now, after his unique path to Antarctica, MIT, and then Haystack, along with his interest in the tools and what they could be used for, a more focused goal emerged. The process was exciting, but it was the end goal of eventually peering at a black hole that kept Shep going.

THE CHASE

|||||||||||||||||||||||||||||||||||||||||||||||||||||||||||||||||||||||||||||||||||||||||||||||||||

Remember how we said if you want to see something that is unimaginably far away, you have to use a really big telescope? Seems simple enough, right? But it's not really. Think of it like this: Imagine using a set of binoculars to look at a faraway mountain. You focus the lenses until you can see individual trees on the mountain. Now, without touching the settings, let's imagine that you turn around to look at your sibling who is standing just across the room from you. Your lens is so powerful that when you look at them with those same mountain-gazing binoculars, you can only see your brother's eyeball!

Luckily, you are pretty familiar with your brother by now, so you know he's more than just that eyeball you see through your binoculars. But if you are making new discoveries or new observations of the cosmos, you are not going to be super familiar with what you are searching for. What if your telescope is so big, so powerful that you only capture a tiny piece of the target? On the other hand, what if your telescope is so small, your target is lost in a giant section of space?

Shep was thinking through that problem. If the telescope was too big, you might only capture a tiny piece of a black hole. Too small? You might not see it at all. How do you figure out the right size of the scope? Shep and his team decided to measure the nearest supermassive black hole.

In 2006, Shep and a small band of fellow astronomers turned their attention to the center of our very own Milky Way galaxy. Like most galaxies, a beastly black hole turns at its center. Shep wanted to measure it. And he was using two radio telescope sites to do it.

The center of the Milky Way galaxy, with the supermassive black hole Sagittarius A* (Sgr A*), located in the middle. The large image contains X-rays from Chandra and infrared emission from the Hubble Space Telescope. The inset shows a close-up view of Sgr A* in X-rays only, covering a region half a light-year wide. (Credit: X-ray: NASA/UMass/D.Wang et al., IR: NASA/STScI)

SAGITTARIUS A*
(pronounced Sagittarius A star or Sag A star)

SHORTHAND: Sgr A*

OBJECT: Supermassive black hole

DISCOVERED: February 13, 1974

RADIUS: 13.67 million miles

MASS: 4 million times the mass of the Sun

DISTANCE FROM EARTH: 25,640 light-years

HOME GALAXY: Milky Way

Step one: Get permission to use radio telescopes in different parts of the world. The farther away they are from one another, the larger the combined telescope becomes. And that means a sharper, more detailed view.

Step two: Each telescope would start recording signals from Sagittarius A* (Sgr A*), the Milky Way's black hole, at the same exact second, collecting light signals and turning them into data that is stored on hard drives.

Step three: Collect the hard drives and combine the data, as if they were all from one giant telescope, providing more detail than would ever be possible from a single scope.

"Nobody had done this before,"[5] Shep said. And if they were successful, it would green-light his ultimate goal: imaging a black hole. Those were the stakes and they were huge. If he was ever going to see a black hole, this had to work.

Shep booked observation time at two of the world's radio telescopes, located in Arizona and Hawaii. The two telescopes would work together to measure the cosmic monster in our neighborhood.

Sitting atop an extinct volcano in Hawaii, Shep knew that both observatories would have to begin recording what they saw at exactly the same time.

"So when we're at the site, we have no idea if things are working, right? It's where we're running purely on trust, purely on the confidence we have in ourselves to set up the experiment perfectly,"[6] Shep explained.

To make sure everything went as smoothly as possible, they walked through the observatory's doors before the sun set, and they stayed awake checking equipment until the sun rose again.

"And we ran these observations and we brought all the data

back to a central facility where they could be combined, effectively creating a virtual telescope as big as the distance between Arizona and Hawaii,"[7] he said.

Instant gratification this was NOT. It would take months of carefully, meticulously going through the data.

Once the team and their data returned to Massachusetts, they began running the data through a supercomputer. Over and over again. Checking and rechecking. It took months to be sure. But finally, they had their results.

And the news was devastating. There were no detections. The experiment was a failure. It was like baking a cake and waiting for it to rise, only to open the oven and discover the oven was not on. Only they couldn't just run to the kitchen for a redo. These telescopes are not just down the street. And time on them is scarce. Scientists compete for these spots. Not to mention all the time, all the money spent. And yet, they had nothing.

They needed to figure out what went wrong. They weren't sure what was to blame. Was it a mechanical failure? A computer glitch? An environmental issue? Something about the black hole itself they didn't understand? No clue. "We didn't know whether nature was being cruel," Shep said.

It was incredibly demoralizing.

"We were just despondent because we put so much energy and time into that experiment," he said.

But eventually they figured it out. One of the telescopes had failed. Plain and simple. And awful.

"If you take these types of things too personally, too deeply, it can damage you,"[8] Shep said. And that was the danger. The sacrifice had been enormous. The amount of work had been intense.

They'd had an incredible amount of brain power. And yet, the experiment failed. It was tough to swallow. There was no getting around it, Shep was sad.

But he was also incredibly driven. And after licking his wounds, he knew it was time to get back up, rally the troops, and take another crack at solving this huge science problem. And that's what got them through it, knowing that they still had not answered the question.

"The most important thing for failure is not that you get up and do it again, but that you learn from your failure," Shep said.

Regrouped and refocused, they got back to work.

The next year, Shep and his team had another shot.

This time they added a third telescope. That way if there was a problem with one telescope, they still had a third to collect data, and it wouldn't be a total loss.

And if all three telescopes were successful, then the team would have more recordings of the signals coming from the center of the Milky Way. More signals meant a more precise view and hopefully, the ability to measure its size.

Once again, they pointed their telescopes to Sgr A* and picked up the radio waves coming from the Milky Way's black hole. Then they brought that data back to Haystack for processing. Once again it would take time to see if it had worked. Had they actually detected the black hole? And gathered enough data to measure it?

Sitting in front of his computer at Haystack, Shep could see the data. The signals, the noise, every bit of data the telescope received was being crunched by the computer, and Shep watched carefully. That's when he noticed that the radio telescopes had picked up on the same signal. All three of them! That could only mean one thing.

They had detected the black hole! "That was probably one of the most amazing experiences I've ever had professionally," he said. "You feel like this pit in your stomach that you're, you're seeing something that nobody else has seen. You are seeing the fruits of years of development and when it works out, it's just exhilarating."[9]

Shep leaped out of his chair and ran back to the supercomputer at the back of the observatory. That's where a man named Mike Titus was working. Shep had to know. Was Mike seeing what he was seeing? The answer was yes!

Getting back up from failure. Learning hard lessons. Regrouping. Moving forward. Trying again. It had all paid off. They published results in one of the biggest scientific journals in the world.

"Everybody's going to fail in their life. You know, in whatever they choose to do, they're going to come up against failure. And if you're not failing, it's because in some sense you're not taking a risk that you need to, to make discoveries," Shep said. "So failure is part of the discovery process, we should welcome it. But, also failure builds your resilience. Maybe if you fail and then you find it within yourself to pick yourself up, dust yourself off and then try again, that's what's really required for great advances."[10]

The Clue Crew

Discovering the possibility of a black hole, thinking about how one might work, and hunting for evidence for black holes was no easy task. But over a span of time, a group of scientists found critical clues, each one passing the torch to the next scientific investigator.

KARL SCHWARZSCHILD

BORN: October 9, 1873

JOB: Astronomer, Physicist

DIED: May 11, 1916

Karl Schwarzschild working in his study at Potsdam. (Credit: AIP Emilio Segrè Visual Archives, courtesy of Martin Schwarzschild)

Karl Schwarzschild grew up in Germany in a busy household as the oldest of six kids. And unlike Shep Doeleman, Karl *did* make his own telescope as a child. By the time Karl was sixteen years old, he was studying the orbits of double stars to understand their orbital paths. He even wrote a scientific paper on his findings and theories, which was published!

Twenty-five years later, his impressive career of studying astronomy and astrophysics was interrupted by World War I. Karl joined the army. While fighting in Russia, Karl noticed blisters on his skin. It was a rare skin disease. But, even though he was at war and in pain, he spent time reading a new theory by Albert Einstein. Einstein had come up with the equations but no clear solutions to them. That's where Karl came in. Working those equations, he realized that Einstein's theory predicted the existence of a black hole. Karl released his solution in 1915 and died just a year later.

This wasn't Schwarzschild's only contribution to science, but it was one of his most famous!

The funny thing was, when scientists read that his mathematical solutions predicted a black hole, they still couldn't quite believe it. Not even Einstein himself. Could it be that this is just where the math ended up on paper, but it didn't actually predict something that existed in our cosmos? It just seemed too bizarre to many scientists.

ROGER PENROSE

BORN: August 8, 1931

JOB: Mathematical Physicist

Roger Penrose was born in England and has devoted his decades-long career to the study of black holes. In 1965 he published a paper showing that according to his mathematical calculations and techniques, black holes absolutely existed—not just on paper, but in real life. Taking a close look at Einstein's theory of general relativity, Penrose showed not only are black holes real, they could actually be formed from dying stars. This evidence was groundbreaking.

In 2004, Penrose penned a book, *The Road to Reality: A Complete Guide to the Laws of the Universe.*

In 2020, Penrose won the Nobel Prize in Physics "for the discovery that black hole formation is a robust prediction of the general theory of relativity."[II] He shared the prize with two other scientists, Andrea Ghez and Reinhard Genzel.

Professor Sir Roger Penrose, January 7, 2011.
(Credit: Biswarup Ganguly)

How about this for a brain bender? Penrose believes that some black holes are left over from previous universes!

STEPHEN HAWKING

BORN: January 8, 1942

JOB: Theoretical Physicist, Mathematician,
Author, Speaker

DIED: March 14, 2018

Stephen Hawking, 1999. (Credit: NASA)

Stephen Hawking was born exactly three hundred years
after Galileo died—to the day. And like Galileo Galilei,
the Father of Observational Astronomy, Hawking would
devote his whole life to investigating the cosmos. Born in
Oxford, England, Hawking was not at the top of his class in
school, but even so, his classmates knew better and called
him "Einstein." As a schoolboy he was already interested
in how things work and took on some of the biggest
questions, like—could God have created the universe? He

BE ON THE LOOKOUT! Stephen Hawking had cameo appearances in several popular TV shows including *Star Trek: The Next Generation, The Big Bang Theory*, and even *The Simpsons*.

made incredible and important contributions to science and our understanding of the cosmos.

Stephen developed many theories about the nature of black holes and their behavior. His theories included the idea that subatomic particles could escape a black hole just before crossing the point of no return. This type of radiation was named Hawking radiation.

Hawking heavily influenced the way black holes were being investigated. Physicists were using general relativity and quantum theory to come up with theories of black holes. But in Hawking's obituary, Roger Penrose (who often worked with Hawking) points out that Hawking realized you also needed to bring in the idea of thermodynamics to really understand how they work. Another of his major contributions was the way he talked to the general public about black holes, the Big Bang theory, and other big ideas. His books made some of the most complicated science easy to understand. These bestselling books made him a household name and made science interesting to masses of people who normally may not have delved into these topics.

BOOKSHELF: *A Brief History of Time* by Stephen Hawking. Stephen's book became a bestseller. He had a talent for writing about complicated ideas in terms everyone could understand.

ANDREA GHEZ

BORN: June 16, 1965

JOB: Astronomer

Andrea Ghez. (Credit: John D. and Catherine T. MacArthur Foundation)

REINHARD GENZEL

BORN: March 24, 1952

JOB: Astronomer

Reinhard Genzel, July 2018. (Credit: ESO/M. Zamani)

It was the Moon landings that got to Andrea Ghez as a child growing up in New York City. Watching human beings walk on the surface of the Moon inspired a love of space. Initially, she wanted to be the first female astronaut, and that interest in exploring other worlds eventually drove her to become an astrophysicist.

Across the Atlantic, Reinhard Genzel lived in Frankfurt, Germany. He was born to physics. His father was a well-known solid-state physicist. When his dad wasn't at work, he showed Reinhard the ropes, often making instruments and conducting experiments. This inspired Reinhard to become an experimental physicist.

Both Ghez and Genzel shared the 2020 Nobel Prize in Physics with Roger Penrose. And they won it for something cool they did in the 1990s. Both astronomers led their own teams to observe stars located in the center of the Milky Way galaxy. While radio signals had been picked up from this location for nearly sixty years, no one knew for sure what the source was. Using powerful telescopes outfitted with a special kind of camera, they tracked and mapped these stars every year for decades. As each orbital movement was captured and compiled, they put the images together into a "movie" for a stunning view. And in 2012, they shared their discovery with the world. These stars were orbiting a massive invisible object. Now they knew that Sagittarius A* could only be one thing: a black hole. Even though they couldn't see it, the stars' behavior gave it away!

CHAPTER 4

HOW TO SEE THE UNSEEABLE

The success of measuring Sagittarius A* was critical. It meant that an Earth-size telescope would work, would be big enough to image a black hole. But how exactly do you capture an image of something that is invisible?

As we've talked about, when we look at stars in the sky, what we are seeing is visible light. We can see only the types of light visible to human eyes, the colors of the rainbow. But that's only part of the picture, and a very small part at that. Luckily, scientists have developed instruments and tools to help us pick up what our eyes can't see.

But wait! If a black hole is . . . well, black—and skulking in the blackness of space, with no light escaping it, how do you see it at all? Well, when it comes to black holes, we know that as material swirls around the accretion disk, it's heated to hundreds of billions of degrees. And that heated material emits radio waves that reach Earth. So radio telescopes could "see" these signals, and if you can see the circle of light that the black hole is bending around its event horizon, then you'll also be able to see a shadow in the center—the black hole itself.

Let's imagine for a minute that a black hole suddenly opened up above your school, high in the sky on a super sunny day. Only you can't see it . . . until it moves in front of the Sun. So now in our fantastical example, the black hole is between the Earth and the Sun. And, against the blinding light of the Sun, suddenly the black hole's black shadow would be visible. Sounds a lot like what it looks like when the Moon travels in front of the Sun creating an eclipse.

That effect is what astronomers thought could make it possible for radio telescopes to pick up a black hole. Only instead of needing a different light source like the Sun, the black hole's own super bright accretion disk would act as the perfect backdrop for the dark shadow of the event horizon. Maybe, if you point a telescope in the right direction, it could pick up that light-filled backdrop, which would also reveal the shadow.

Think about sitting in a stadium watching a soccer match. If your seats are far away from the field, the soccer players appear tiny, and the ball they are chasing is even smaller. Now think about trying to see something that's millions of light-years away . . .

"The entire reason this hasn't been done," Shep explained, "is that black holes are extremely small. It would be the equivalent of trying to see an orange at the distance of the moon."[12]

And it's weird to say "small" when you are talking about a gigantic, supermassive black hole. But from where we stand here on Earth, the black hole appears impossibly small. So small and so far away we can't see it with our eyes, even if we had special goggles on to help us perceive the full spectrum of light. Bottom line? The size of the telescope needs to be huge. But how can you build and use a telescope dish the size of Earth itself? Earth's diameter alone is 7,926.2 miles!

> **BRAIN BENDER!** Wait, how big is Earth exactly? If you put a measuring tape around Earth at the equator, the circumference is 24,901 miles. Earth's surface comes in at 197 million square miles! Earth may look like a perfectly round sphere, but the radius at the poles is thirteen miles less than at the equator. So, what do you call that shape? An oblate spheroid.

The answer? Use Very Long Baseline Interferometry to create a virtual telescope by connecting telescopes around the world and pointing them at the same object. Shep's previous project had created a telescope the size of the distance between Arizona and Hawaii. What if he could make a network of radio telescopes as big as Earth itself?

"By spanning the globe, you create a new kind of instrument that can see a black hole,"[13] Shep said. They were pushing VLBI to its limit. This technology had never been used for this.

"You need telescopes around the world. You need the expertise and goodwill of people from around the world, so you have to cultivate that. And, and in a project like the horizon telescope, the important thing for me was that we cultivated our own culture,"[14] Shep said.

If they succeeded not only would they add to the human knowledge of the cosmos, but the idea itself, of using an Earth-size telescope, could be repurposed to investigate other enormous cosmic questions. And that was exciting. This reality sharpened

Shep's already laser-like focus to an even finer point. It came down to this question, "What do we have to do to make this happen?"[15]

There were many challenges to this idea. One, the world only has a handful of radio telescopes. Getting time on them is competitive. Two, these radio telescopes were located in some of the most remote places on Earth. Three, they were not designed to be used like this. They would have to be fitted with special (and expensive) equipment in order to work together. Four, this would require an unprecedented level of global cooperation and collaboration during a time when the world seemed to be retreating into conflict and division at every turn. Could this team be the exception?

And then, once they had the data—enormous, almost unfathomable amounts of data—then what? They would have to process it. So, five, they needed supercomputers capable of handling the data, hard drives capable of storing the data, and a plan for taking all that data and translating it into an image.

The truth was, the computing power required to record their observations and then make sense of them didn't exist yet. But, Shep was willing to bet that, since computing had already developed so quickly, it would continue to improve, and just in time to handle their data. That was a major gamble.

Oh, and finally, six, all of this costs money. A lot of money. Millions of dollars. So, you need that, too.

These were big questions. Big problems to solve. But, Shep still believed it was possible. So, he and his growing team wasted no time diving into the deep end to solve them.

The 411 on M87's Black Hole

When you look up at the night sky, at the Virgo constellation, you are looking at a black hole. It's swirling right in the heart of a galaxy called M87.

People can't see it with their tiny, limited human eyes. After all, it's 55 million light-years away. And it's invisible to us. But it's there. And it's not just any ole black hole. It's a supermassive black hole with the mass of 6.5 billion suns.

LIGHT SPEED: The speed of light is 186,000 miles a second.

ACCRETION DISK SPEED: Two million miles per hour. The inside of the accretion disk is zooming around faster than the outer bits.

JET: Black Hole Jets are on the cutting edge of black hole research. There is so much to learn about them and how they work. Scientists have used multiple types of telescopes to study these jets including optical, radio, and x-ray. So, what have they learned? As material swirls around the black hole, some of it is slung right into the event horizon never to be seen again. But some of this material is shot away from the black hole in powerful jets. If you had a cosmic speed gun, you could clock these jets at nearly the speed of light. The jets can travel far, too! Some have traveled 5,000 light-years!

A black-hole-powered jet of subatomic particles streaming out from the center of M87. (Credit: NASA and the Hubble Heritage Team (STScI/AURA))

CHAPTER 5

HELP IS ON THE WAY

Across the Atlantic, another scientist had been investigating the same question for a number of years: Was it possible to take a picture of a black hole?

His name was Dr. Heino Falcke. And in 2013, he named his project Black Hole Cam. The name makes it sound like Heino had a webcam ready to point at a black hole and take its picture. Nothing could have been further from the truth. It was simply a snappy name for an unbelievably complicated idea, just like Shep's.

Heino's main job was as professor of radio astronomy and astroparticle physics at Radboud University. He was successful, winning awards, building his reputation, and eventually winning a multimillion-euro prize. This prize focused on Heino's work in investigating black holes and building telescopes in Northern Europe.

RADBOUD UNIVERSITY is a Roman Catholic university. Located in the Netherlands, this research university is ranked as one of the best in the world. Students, professors, and staff research scientists are often engaged in groundbreaking science. The school's mission is to contribute to a "healthy, free world with equal opportunities for all."[16] The university was founded in 1923 to provide opportunities for Catholics who were shut out of research positions, medical careers, and legal careers during that time due to anti-Catholic bigotry.

Goudsmit pavilion and Huygens building, Radboud University, Nijmegen, the Netherlands. (Credit: Bj.schoenmakers)

Heino's path to radio astronomy began when he was a small boy. He was obsessed with the garbage truck that passed by his Cologne, Germany, home.

He didn't want to simply watch the truck, he dreamed of becoming a garbage truck driver. All these years later he still tells the tale with glee and adoration.

"I was playing on the street. I was five or six years old. There were big garbage trucks driving by every week,"[17] he said, unable to hide the joy of this memory. He remembers watching the workers. They climbed out of the truck and pressed buttons on its side. And suddenly, metal arms would lower to grab the cans, then lift them up and dump the trash into the truck. Not only that, but, to his amazement, the driver pushed another button. And that one smashed the garbage together. He was smitten with the machinery. With just a push of a few buttons, a big machine could accomplish incredible things. The machinery!

But machinery wasn't the only thing that caught Heino's attention: He was also interested in the big questions of life, of existence, of the very nature of time itself.

One question in particular kept him up night after night.

"I was thinking about 'heaven' and what does that mean. And I was wondering what's behind heaven? And if there is something behind it, what's behind that? I

Heino Falcke, age six. (Photo courtesy of Heino Falcke)

was trying to grapple with the concept of infinity," he explained. "Trying to understand infinity was really mind blowing to me."

Raised in a devout Christian family, Heino was curious about God, too. "And luckily I grew up in an environment where I was allowed to ask questions." He remembers reading the Bible and simultaneously asking lots of questions . . . always about the nature of God, the nature of infinity.

BOOKSHELF: When Heino was growing up, he read the magazine *Scientific American* in German. "I was fascinated by particle physics and astrophysics. I was very curious all the time,"[18] he said.

Answering those big questions led to a career in science, in astronomy.

When he was getting his PhD, he worked with 100-meter radio telescopes. Huge machines. And the first time he pressed the buttons, it brought him right back to when he was a small boy, watching the garbage truck.

"I was pressing gate buttons and the thing would move and I felt like a garbage truck driver!"[19]

Heino Falcke at the IRAM 30m on Pico Veleta, Spain. (Photo courtesy of Heino Falcke, © Salvador Sanchez)

Shep and Heino found themselves at the same place and time in 2013, at an astronomy conference in Santa Fe, New Mexico. The conference was focused on one thing: the center of galaxies.

TYPES OF GALAXIES: In 1936, astronomer Edwin Hubble, for whom the Hubble Telescope is named, debuted a way for scientists to classify galaxies based on their shape and size.

ELLIPTICAL GALAXIES: These elliptical-shaped galaxies make up some of the largest in the known universe, even containing up to a trillion stars!

SPIRAL GALAXY: Our galaxy, the Milky Way, is a spiral galaxy, looking like a whirligig spinning through space with spiraling arms and a bulge at the center. There are subcategories like the Barred Spiral Galaxy Shape: This galaxy has spiraling arms, but the central bulge appears fixed in the middle of a glowing bar. This gives it an S shape.

LENTICULAR GALAXIES: These look like lenses. They are round, flat disks.

IRREGULAR GALAXIES: A catch-all category for the galaxies that have odd shapes or don't have a clear form.

Shep had been hard at work on his idea about how to build a telescope that could peer into the darkest corner of the universe: a black hole. And he'd been building a team of people from around the world to help him.

Heino's idea was very similar to Shep's idea. Radio telescopes would link together and aim for a black hole. After all, it would be a great opportunity to test Einstein's theories. That was exciting to Heino.

They were on to something. But not all of the technology they needed existed. Still, Shep was as convinced as he'd always been that if history was any indicator, the speed of advancements in computer technology would continue to grow. His crew was committed to solving the technological problems. Plus, Shep's breakthroughs were now widely reported in the press and academic journals.

Heino's accomplishments, his steady progress, advancements and published papers, and his position at Radboud gave him a lot of academic prestige, too. And in the world and culture of astronomy, that mattered a lot.

And there was this. Even though Shep had already put in years modifying ALMA, that did not guarantee telescope time. Located in the Chilean desert on a plateau in the Andes Mountains, above water vapor, ALMA was one of the most important telescopes in

Antennae of the Atacama Large Millimeter/submillimeter Array (ALMA), on the Chajnantor Plateau in the Chilean Andes. (Credit: ESO/C. Malin)

the world. And that telescope was essential for getting an image of a black hole, because ALMA had sixty-six antennae, which would add way more detail to any image. "The crown jewel is ALMA," Shep said. "The effective size of it is about a 90-meter dish—which is mind-blowing." It was the biggest array at the best location. EHT needed ALMA. "It happens to be one of the best sites to observe at these frequencies on the planet," he said.

But a hallmark of ALMA's existence is a spirit of worldwide collaboration. Not competition. Having Heino and his growing European team on board as part of EHT would demonstrate the depth of commitment to global collaboration. And that would give them access to observation time at ALMA. The path was clear. These two teams needed to work together if they wanted to see the unseeable.

Shep's career path was intentionally different. He wanted to work on telescopes and build an Earth-size telescope. That was his singular focus. He was banking his entire career on this one thing. He was comfortable being the underdog, the outsider, who was driven to accomplish his goal. And he was building a team to get it done.

Neither effort was a secret, certainly not in the science world. Science reporters wrote about both. It was time to take this idea to the next level fast. But the two teams had a decision to make.

Should they join forces and work together to solve these problems? Or should they race against each other, competing to be the first, and taking all the credit? Or would they miss out entirely because they couldn't get ALMA on board?

The truth was they needed each other. Heino could bring his expertise and funding sources, and grow the global nature of the team. And Shep and his team brought a world of experience, having chased down technological problems and done the work required to build the instrument capable of doing this job. They both had technical expertise and leadership qualities. And to accomplish what seemed impossible to most people, these two teams needed every possible advantage. Plain and simple, if the world wanted to see a black hole, the world was going to have to work together.

Heino and his own team of brilliant scientists and mathematicians decided to join Shep's Event Horizon Telescope project.

"We all were united by a common vision and that we knew how important it was,"[20] Shep said.

As Heino summed it up, "There is nothing as exciting as an open question."[21]

Now it was time to answer it.

Meet the Team!
Part 1

There were more than three hundred people involved in this project. Let's meet just a few!

LAURA VERTATSCHITSCH is a brilliant electrical engineer and advanced radar systems expert. For EHT, she helped build the digital recorders required during their observation. But she also wowed the team with her performance of a song she wrote. It was a love song to black holes!

JONATHAN WEINTROUB, originally from South Africa, was the first radio astronomer to join the Event Horizon Telescope project with Shep. Affiliated with the Smithsonian Astrophysical Observatory / Harvard-Smithsonian Center for Astrophysics, Jonathan brought a lot of expertise to the effort, including having built a correlator, the equipment required to combine readings from multiple telescopes.

RAMESH NARAYAN is a polymath researcher at the Harvard-Smithsonian Center for Astrophysics. His area of focus was on understanding how black holes feed!

FERYAL ÖZEL was born in Istanbul, Turkey. She is an astronomer at the University of Arizona and was critical in leading a team to create computer simulations that would help the team identify the best observation windows.

6

SHOW ME THE MONEY

If you've ever taken on a big science project, I mean the kind that could win the science fair, it's gonna take some money. After all, you have to have supplies, both to conduct the experiment and for your display and presentation. Well, this was a science project on steroids. And it required money.

Some of the telescopes needed new equipment. They needed upgrades. And many of the telescopes were located in the world's most extreme environments. Travel was expensive. The team would also need to hire more scientists, researchers, engineers, and support staff. They needed more time on the telescopes. They needed atomic clocks to keep extraordinarily precise time. And basic expenses like office supplies and food. The list grew and grew, and the cost grew with it.

The total price tag would be around $60 million. That was a lot of money—maybe not an enormous amount in terms of big science bets, but it was definitely more than Shep and his team had access to.

No money? No chasing black holes. Shep knew that without funding, actual money, this dream of taking a pic of a black hole had no chance of becoming reality.

And they couldn't just knock on the local bank's door and ask for it either. They had to apply for grants. They had to explain the problem they were trying to solve, how they planned to solve it, how the money would be spent, what the impact would be on science. Their explanation had to be detailed and thorough. They had to think through every question someone might have about their project and be sure to answer it. Then their application was carefully reviewed by serious experts. And then, a decision.

Detecting gravitational waves was a Nobel Prize–winning success for the LIGO project. But it came with a hefty price tag: $1.1 billion. The Hubble Telescope that's captured iconic images of space cost $9.6 billion.

They needed millions of dollars to conduct the experiment, and success was not a certainty. They could spend all of that money and the project could still fail.

It was a major risk. But the payoff could be huge for science and for humanity. Who would pay for something like this?

Shep received smaller grants from places like the Gordon and

Betty Moore Foundation, the Smithsonian Astrophysical Observatory, MIT, and others. But they still needed big money.

Shep turned to the National Science Foundation (NSF), and applied for a $7 million grant. The NSF is a government-funded agency that analyzes and funds some of the biggest research projects on the planet. Even risky ones, like Shep's, that centered on innovation and breaking new ground. The risk was enormous. But so was the potential reward.

Not only could the image itself possibly get the world's attention, but it could offer definitive proof of black holes . . . the seeing-is-believing kind of proof.

Having the NSF behind the project would be huge. The science was going to be incredibly difficult. And keeping the project funded would not be a walk in the park either. NSF Director Dr. France Córdova explained why. "You can't do it all by yourself because the forces are too big and they just clobber you,"[22] France said. She went on to say that whether it's roadblocks from Congress or the White House or naysayers in the public, obstacles can and will pop up.

"We have the kind of organization where we say, 'No, we believe these people. They have good arguments for doing this.' We have reviewed it and reviewed it,"[23] France explained.

BOOKSHELF: The Nancy Drew mysteries by Carolyn Keene. These books were France Córdova's favorites as a young woman. "If you had asked me what I wanted to be at that age," she explained, "I would have said a detective . . . mysteries just really intrigued me and I consider science full of mysteries. And I think I *am* a detective."

Meanwhile, Heino had applied for a multimillion-dollar grant from the European Research Council Synergy Grants. Just like the science would be a global effort, paying the bills would be a global effort, too. Heino and his team were up against eight hundred other worthy applicants. Once they made it into the finals, they even had to show up for an in-person interview in Brussels. But, finally, they received the grant!

Yet, Shep was still waiting. Just when he thought his proposal was going to be completely rejected, his phone rang. The NSF grant was his!

Suddenly, the Event Horizon Telescope project had a real chance of coming together. And as the project grew, financial support came in from institutions in Taiwan, Germany, Mexico, Japan, Canada, the United States, Italy, Spain, China, Korea, South Africa, Russia, Sweden, and more. The National Science Foundation would fund the largest share, ultimately totaling more than $26 million.

Got Questions?

Is it possible to make something invisible? How big was that ancient megalodon, really? Can ripples in space-time be detected? What does the surface of the Sun really look like? Is there evidence of the Big Bang? If only 80 percent of the ocean has been explored, what else is there to discover in the deepest parts of the sea?

Exploring these questions requires money to pay for things like travel, trained scientists, supplies, laboratories, equipment, and support while you try to achieve a scientific breakthrough. And providing that money and support is what the National Science Foundation (NSF) is most passionate about. The NSF was started back in 1950 when the United States Congress wanted to make sure that America made major progress in all areas of science. Given a multibillion-dollar budget, the NSF receives proposals from scientists on a variety of projects and decides which investigations to fund, based on which projects will advance America's scientific research.

So, is it possible to make something invisible? Yes! With NSF funding scientists have been able to do this in the lab and are investigating how to apply this cool trick elsewhere. This research is still in early stages, but maybe one day soon an invisibility cloak could go into production!

And what about ocean exploration? Meet *Alvin*! That's the name of a deep-sea submersible that can explore depths of up to fifteen thousand feet. Human pilots guide *Alvin* as it explores two thirds of the ocean floor, making discoveries like hydrothermal vents!

Can you determine an ancient shark's size, when it lived 3.6 million years ago? Yes! Paleobiologists, in an NSF-funded study, came up with a math equation that uses the length of the shark's teeth to nail down their body length. The megalodon was an astonishing 50 feet long—that's as wide as a basketball court!

And check out this picture of the surface of the Sun! It was taken with an NSF solar telescope. This photo shows more detail of the surface of the Sun than ever seen before and can be used to understand solar weather, or how what's happening on the Sun's surface affects life here on Earth. The goal of this research is to expand what we know about our very own star!

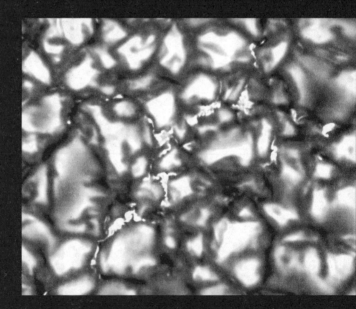

The Daniel K. Inouye Solar Telescope has produced the highest-resolution image of the Sun's surface ever taken. In this picture, taken at 789 nanometers (nm), we can see features as small as 30km (18 miles) in size for the first time ever. The image shows a pattern of turbulent, "boiling" gas that covers the entire Sun. The cell-like structures—each about the size of Texas—are the signature of violent motions that transport heat from the inside of the Sun to its surface.
(Credit: NSO/AURA/NSF)

In this first image alone, you can see the surface is covered in boiling plasma. Each little kernel-like shape is actually the size of the state of Texas. Could images like these help scientists better predict space weather? That's the goal!

These are just a tiny sample of the kinds of questions and research topics the National Science Foundation (NSF) explores.

7

CLIMB THE HIGHEST MOUNTAIN

Earth's atmosphere is a problem. It's full of water. The very thing that sustains us is a thorn in the side of a radio astronomer. The part of the water cycle that fills our planet's skies with water vapor also does something else ... absorbs and scatters microwaves before they ever hit the telescope dish on the ground.

So, to minimize that effect and catch as many of those rays as possible, you want radio telescopes built at high altitudes where the air is thin and water vapor isn't a problem, which means traveling to remote areas, climbing tall mountains, and going to other extremes just to get to these telescopes.

The EHT team needed to expand and tweak their network of three telescope sites in Hawaii, Arizona, and California to eight observatories around the globe—located in Spain, Mexico, Arizona, Hawaii, Chile, and the South Pole. These eight sites were located between seven thousand and sixteen thousand feet above sea level. Perfect spots for lower air density and little water vapor.

"You are linking telescopes that are ten thousand kilometers apart,"[24] Shep told a documentary crew from his home institution, the Smithsonian. This was going to require true technological innovation. VLBI had never been used like this, on this scale, for this purpose. In order for it to work, their timing had to reach a level of precision that's hard to wrap your mind around. Otherwise the data would be a meaningless jumble. The coordination of these telescopes had to be perfect. Period.

And that meant the team needed to travel to each of these telescope sites. This wasn't easy physical work. But doing so would allow scientists to look at a black hole with the same resolution required to take a picture of an orange on the surface of the Moon or, another example, the ability to climb to the top of the Empire State building in New York City and read a newspaper lying on a café table in London!

None of the telescopes were built specifically for the Event Horizon Telescope project. And since they were pushing the technology to its limit, the telescopes needed to be retrofitted with mirrors to focus the radio waves and point them at the telescopes' receivers. They also needed maser clocks—some of the most precise clocks in the world, which are accurate down to a ten-thousandth of a millionth of a millionth of a second over the course of one year. Bottom line? It's a super accurate timekeeping dynamo.

Looking at the temperature, EHT physicist Dan Marrone braced himself. The windchill outside was minus seventy degrees. He was working on the South Pole Telescope. It was the most difficult to travel to and the weather conditions were nothing to laugh at. But having that telescope on board would double the resolution of the image.

The South Pole Telescope in docking position during EHT preparations in January 2017. (Credit: Daniel Michalik / South Pole Telescope)

DAN MARRONE: Experimental Astrophysicist at the University of Arizona. He is especially interested in galaxy clusters, galaxy formation, and Sagittarius A*!

The telescope was made to study aspects of the Big Bang. Dan needed to install a new receiver. When cosmic objects emit light of any kind, if those rays make it to Earth, telescopes collect the light. New mirrors for the South Pole Telescope (SPT) would receive light and focus on the telescope's original mirrors, which would then send the signal directly to the new receiver. Once the work was done, the telescope had to be tested to make sure everything was working correctly. From installation to testing, the work took fifty days without a single day off. But he got the job done.

The telescope in Mexico would require new digital equipment for EHT's purposes. It was nerve-racking. Maser clocks cost around $300,000. And this one had to be attached to a cable and pulled up a spiral staircase before it was put in position.

Scientists perform what is effectively a "heart transplant" on the ALMA correlator by installing a custom-built atomic clock powered by a hydrogen maser. (Credit: Carlos Padilla, NRAO/AUI/NSF)

At the observatory site in Chile, called ALMA (which is short for Atacama Large Millimeter/submillimeter Array), there was an array of sixty-six antennae. And light from cosmic objects hits each of these sixty-six antennae at slightly different times. Kind of like if you and your family are slightly spread out in the backyard, waiting for the sprinkler to spray you with water. You'll all be sprayed, even if you are standing in a row directly under the stream of water. But if your sister is closer to the sprinkler, the water will hit her first.

This aerial picture shows the Chajnantor Plateau, location of the ALMA Observatory, from high above. Dozens of dishes from the observatory are spread over the plateau and cast long dark shadows in the red sand. In the center of the image the crowded gathering of the Atacama Compact Array is visible. (Credit: ALMA (ESO/NAOJ/NRAO), A. Marinkovic/X-Cam)

Every antenna in this array links to a supercomputer, which aligns the signals and correlates the data in a process called phasing. Out of all the radio telescopes on the planet, this was the most powerful. ALMA's array was extremely sensitive and adding this site to EHT meant the resolution would increase by a factor of ten. But for EHT to be able to effectively use this site, Shep led a team to develop and install new hardware and software, including digital recorders. The observation site and the recorders were sixteen miles away from each other. So they would need to add a fiber-optic link system as well.

This task required something else, too: absolute belief in the goal and a vision for how to accomplish it. And Shep delivered on that essential ingredient. All the way back in 2011, when Shep first thought about a global network of telescopes, he understood how critical AMLA would be in actually having a shot at imaging a black hole. So he turned to the NSF for funding. In 2016, some five years later, the modifications were complete. Just in time!

They could now program this array to conduct VLBI experiments to observe the submillimeter spectrum of light. And what was really exciting was, when the EHT team figured out how to tweak this system, not only did it bring them closer to their own goal, it also helped the greater science community who could use VLBI to explore other cosmic mysteries.

Telescope by telescope, they were devising a network that was sensitive enough to make out the inner ring of a black hole. Finally, the technology had caught up. They tested each site. It worked. The telescopes could connect effectively and act as one. They were in a position to really take a shot at imaging a black hole.

Telescope Tour, Part 1

SOUTH POLE TELESCOPE (SPT)

LOCATION: Antarctica

ALTITUDE: 9,300 feet

The southern lights (aurora australis) over the South Pole Telescope.
(Credit: Joshua Montgomery)

Submillimeter Array (SMA)

LOCATION: Maunakea, Hawaii

ALTITUDE: 13,386 feet

*All eight antennae of the Submillimeter Array in nighttime observation.
(Credit: Nimesh Patel)*

Atacama Large Millimeter/ submillimeter Array (ALMA)

LOCATION: Atacama Desert, Chile

ALTITUDE: 16,400 feet

*Snowy sunrise at the Chajnantor Plateau with ALMA.
(Credit: NAOJ/NRAO/ESO)*

ATACAMA PATHFINDER EXPERIMENT (APEX)

LOCATION: Atacama Desert, Chile

ALTITUDE: 17,000 feet

Sunset over the Atacama Desert, Chile, the home of the APEX observatory. (Credit: Sven Dornbusch)

CHAPTER 8

DO YOU WANT TO
BUILD A SNOWMAN?

Fifth-grade science fan Katie Bouman stood next to her project. Her experiment had nothing to do with black holes. No, Katie was focused on bread, specifically "how the taste and the rise of bread was affected by the different kinds of yeast, salt, and sugar combinations you put in it,"[25] she explained.

She knew her experiment inside out. She was prepared for any question, and the details of her process were at the ready. She could basically take anything that was thrown at her.

"I was always more into projects than paper-and-pen kind of homework,"[26] Katie said.

And so, standing there at her science fair, Katie was beyond excited.

Beaming, she discovered that she loved it, everything about doing science, the process of asking a question, and investigating until you found an answer or more questions. Though love doesn't seem a strong enough word. Devotion. Passion. Fascination. All rolled up into one.

Katie may have only been in the fifth grade, attending her first science fair. But this was the moment when she knew. The moment she stepped on the beginning of her scientific journey. She had the chance to present her work at the Purdue Science Fair. And she won the gold medal for her category.

"I was like on top of the world after that,"[27] she said.

Katie Bouman at her ninth-grade science fair. (Photo courtesy of Katie Bouman)

In ninth grade, it was fingerprint analysis that captured her attention. "I would take images of fingerprints and I came up with methods and determined genetic similarities across people using their fingerprint pattern,"[28] she said.

By the tenth grade, she knew she wanted to work on science on her own. She contacted Purdue University directly asking to work with a professor who was studying how people perceive color. Katie wanted to investigate whether there was a measurable difference in how, for example, you see the color blue and how your best friend sees it. Are you seeing the same color or two different colors? Does the way we learn about colors and label colors affect what we describe as blue or red or green? At its heart, the project was zeroing in on what our brain does with data on color and how we interpret that data in describing it.

That project cemented Katie's interest in the type of scientific problem solving that required new thinking and new tools. It also solidified her interest in imaging. How do you use imaging to find the answers? Spending so many hours in a laboratory that processed video and images only fanned the flames of her curiosity.

Years later, Katie was working on her PhD, with a focus on imaging. She wanted to understand how our brain works when it comes to seeing and understanding material properties. "Let's say you have a woman and she's walking towards you, right? And she's wearing a dress. If you watch the dress blowing in the wind, you can usually tell, is it corduroy or is it silk? You can get some idea of the material properties from it,"[29] she said.

She was excited because humans can generally tell the difference when fabric is moving. But what if there were hidden vibrations or other information that humans can't see or notice?

That really piqued her interest: getting more information by using imaging to see things that humans can't . . . or that humans can't see fully.

Think about walking through your house—you notice the color of the walls, the carpet, the pictures on the wall. But if a firefighter comes to your house looking for fire, they would use a special camera that picks up heat. This camera is NOT concerned with the color of the walls . . . it's only imaging heat. So, if you take your hand and touch the wall, the heat from your handprint will show up in the image! These special heat-sensing cameras allow firefighters to find smoldering fires behind the walls so that they can snuff them out before the entire house burns down.

In a similar way, most things that humans *see* are only part of the picture. What Katie was excited about was looking for that hidden story. What else was there, hidden from human eyes, waiting to be discovered?

Katie Bouman sitting in the APEX LMT telescope.
(Photo courtesy of Katie Bouman)

Then, in 2014, when Katie heard Shep talk about the Event Horizon Telescope project, what they were trying to do, she knew she could help. She was not an astrophysicist, but this project would require imaging, and more than that, a unique use of computational imaging.

"I just thought it was interesting. It brought together a lot of areas that I was interested in," she said. "I mean, what's cooler than working on black holes?"[30] Katie talked to Shep and other members of the team. She quickly realized that coming up with the math and algorithms to support the project was going to take a much bigger team. They were going to need mathematicians *and* engineers *and* astrophysicists to work together in order to observe and image the black hole. Experts with different areas of expertise from around the globe were coming together to solve this problem—what a unique and very exciting opportunity.

It was also going to be hard. After all, what they were doing had never been done before or even attempted.

Katie and her colleagues had to figure out how to take the EHT data from the radio telescopes and turn it into an image, a true picture that would allow humans to actually *see* a black hole for the first time. They practiced on synthetic data. If they were all given the same set of data, one that should make the image of a mystery shape, could they use algorithms to come up with the same image? Would human bias affect their work? They tried many different approaches, and eventually, using blind data, each team produced the same result: a snowman.

Katie and her team were so excited. They were perfecting a plan, and they wanted to be ready as soon as the data was.

INTERSTELLAR

Remember astrophysicist John Archibald Wheeler who gave black holes their name? He was a teacher as well, and one of his students was astrophysicist Kip Thorne, the man who would later use real science to create the computer-generated black hole named Gargantua in the 2014 movie *Interstellar*. Dr. Thorne is a professor emeritus of physics at California Institute of Technology (Caltech).

When Katie joined the team in 2014, *Interstellar* had just hit theaters. So Katie and part of the team went to see the movie. Everyone got there late and they couldn't sit together. But still, she was there at *Interstellar* watching Matthew McConaughey's intergalactic travels, with some of the world's leading black hole experts who were embarking on a real-life quest to see a black hole.

"*Interstellar* made it possible to basically have the high-resolution imagery of a black hole. Of course, they did take some artistic liberty with it . . . simulating a thin disc around the black hole rather than a puffy kind of disc that we expect to see,"[31] she explained.

When the movie ended and the lights came on, Katie wondered if her astrophysicist colleagues were going to pick it apart and tell her everything that was wrong with it. "And so we got out of the movie and I remember my friend Michael Johnson, he just, like, came over to us and he was, like, that was awesome. And I thought that was just great. They're just such a fun crew."[32]

CHAPTER 9

GO TIME

Finally, on April 4, 2017, the moment had arrived. After all the planning, retrofitting, funding, relationship building, problem solving . . . after all of that . . . it was time to carry out the experiment.

Sitting in the middle of ten computers, Shep got to work. While EHT teams filled the eight observatories around the world, Shep was running central command in Cambridge, Massachusetts, at the Black Hole Initiative. Through webcams, chats, and conference calls, Shep was ready to work through any problem and answer any question that came up. The makeshift command center was small but efficient.

At the Black Hole Initiative in Cambridge, MA, during observations. Left to right: Lia Medeiros, Shep Doeleman, Kazunori Akiyama, Vincent Fish, Jim Moran, Feryal Ozel. (Credit: EHT)

On one wall was a whiteboard that would tell the tale. A dry-erase chart was drawn onto it with a sort of checklist for each observatory location. How that chart was filled in would be the key to everything. No matter how ready the computers were, no matter how sharp the scientists, if the weather didn't cooperate the whole effort could fail. And it was completely out of their control.

The observation window was just ten days long. If they were going to see M87* (M87 star) and Sagittarius A*, then they had only ten days to do it. The more days they were able to make observations, the more data they would have. But, the more days they had to cancel due to a problem at any of the sites, the less data they would have to work with. In order to make an image, they needed at least four successful nights. Period. And, of course, the telescopes themselves had to work perfectly. The data recording also could not fail. The pressure was intense.

Dry-erase marker in hand, Shep was ready. Location by location. Technical difficulty, yes or no? Good weather? Yes or no? And every day at 4:00 p.m. (EST), Shep would make the call: go, or no go. The observation window would open the next day. The team was ready.

April 5, 2017, Spain (where Heino was spending the ten days while enjoying the amazing food that local residents brought up to feed the hungry scientists) passed the test for technical readiness and clear weather. Chile, Arizona, Hawaii, and Mexico also got check marks for technical and weather. The South Pole was out due to technical difficulties. But everyone else was passing the test. Shep sent out a message to the entire team, "GO . . ."[33]

IRAM's Pico Veleta VLBI crew. Left to right: Salvador, Rebecca, Ignazio, Heino, Thomas. (Credit: Salvador Sanchez)

In Cambridge, they counted down the final five seconds before the computers began recording out loud, like you would for a rocket launch, "Five. Four. Three. Two. One."

As Earth continued to spin, different sites began recording as their position on the planet lined up to observe the targets. Heino reported from Spain that it was going well. And suddenly the South Pole station's technical problems appeared to be fixed. They were all able to observe.

April 6, 2017

Technical readiness? Check! Weather? Check! Wait! The observatory in Mexico—not looking good on either front. The power was going in and out at the observatory and there was a chance for bad weather that could deposit a serious chunk of ice on the dish. Shep spent much of the day talking to the team, trying to troubleshoot. His 4:00 p.m. (EST) deadline came and went. Forty minutes later Shep sent the message to the team. It was a GO.

April 7, 2017

No Go.

April 8, 2017

No Go.

April 9, 2017

No Go.

April 10, 2017

Weather? Yes.

Technical? Yes.

Go!

April 11, 2017

Weather? Yes.

Technical? Yes.

Go!

The worldwide team now included more than three hundred scientists, mathematicians, and engineers from fifty-nine institutions like universities and research centers in twenty different countries. The global collaboration was impressive, especially against a backdrop of headlines like the Ebola outbreak in West Africa, fighting in Ukraine and Crimea, Israel and Palestine on the brink of war, protests in Hong Kong, the rise of ISIS (a new terror group that would soon become a household name), riots in the United States over police brutality against Black people—against all of that, these teams were working together, accumulating sixty-five hours of observation time to push forward humanity's understanding of the cosmos.

At the end of ten days, they had four nights of observations total, exactly what they needed. All together, they acquired six million gigabytes of data.

Celebration at LMT after an observation run. Left to right: Antonio Hernández, Sergio Dzib, Emir Moreno, Edgar Castillo, Gopal Narayanan, Katie Bouman, and Sandra Bustamante. (Credit: Ana Torres Campos)

"The fact that everything worked. The weather was perfect," Heino marveled. "It was as good as it ever had been before, in the decade before, and maybe as good as it ever will be in the next ten years . . . at all the sites around the world!"[34]

For Shep it was a full-circle moment. He remembered when he was a kid trying to see the eclipse and the clouds parted at just the right moment so he could see something that is normally invisible to us. Had that happened again? Had the team captured the invisible? What would it reveal?

Telescope Tour, Part 2

IRAM 30M

LOCATION: Pico Veleta, Spain

ALTITUDE: 9,400 feet

IRAM 30-meter telescope in snow under the moonlight.
(Credit: IRAM, N. Billot)

James Clerk
Maxwell Telescope

LOCATION: Maunakea, Hawaii

ALTITUDE: 13,400 feet

JCMT while observing at night with telescope covered.
(Credit: EAO, William Montgomerie)

LARGE MILLIMETER TELESCOPE ALFONSO SERRANO (LMT)

LOCATION: Sierra Negra, Mexico
(atop an extinct volcano)

ALTITUDE: 15,220 feet

Large Millimeter Telescope "Alfonso Serrano" with completed 50-meter surface pointing upward at sunset. (Credit: INAOE Archives)

SUBMILLIMETER TELESCOPE (SMT)

LOCATION: Mt. Graham, Arizona

ALTITUDE: 10,500 feet

The Submillimeter Telescope open for observations under the starry sky. (Credit: Dave Harvey)

10

RISE ABOVE THE NOISE

Now it was time to leave the telescopes, fly the data to Haystack and Bonn, Germany, and find out if it worked.

And, as Shep knew well, getting the data out of Antarctica would take months. They had five petabytes of data—way too much to send over the internet. It's hard to visualize, but as Dan Marrone explained, you can think of it like this—if you listened to music on an MP3 player, you'd have to listen for five thousand years to get through just as much data! Another example of Dan's? They collected enough data to equal "all of the selfies that forty thousand people will take in their lifetime."[35]

The only way to transport that much data was to fly it out. But, it was the dead of winter there. Planes would not be able to safely land or take off for five more months. Even though the team would start processing the other data as quickly as possible, the complete dataset could not be correlated and combined until then.

The last data from the EHT observations in April 2017. Each module holds eight hard disks with a total capacity of 64 Terabytes. (Credit: MIT Haystack Observatory)

And combining the data was only the beginning. They would also need to sift out the actual signals from all the other meaningless noise that was recorded. Then all of that data would need to be validated. And only after all of that would the imaging teams begin interpreting the data. So, anyone looking for an immediate answer as to whether this whole global exercise had been a success? They would just have to wait.

The team had observed both Sgr A* and M87* and for different reasons. They decided they would try to get an image from M87's black hole. "The issue with Sgr A*, it's a thousand times smaller. It's a thousand times closer so it has the same shadow size. But it's also a thousand times faster. So if you want to take an image of that source, it's like taking an image of a toddler who moves around for eight hours and you are trying to get a still image,"[36] Heino Falcke explained to reporters.

"We really are taking voyages to these black holes, in the case of M87, fifty-five million light-years away," Shep said. "And then we're creating instruments, we're devising algorithms, we are taking observations to bring the black hole to life, to show us what a black hole really looks like and then we have to return back and describe it to everyone."[37] That was the goal. But had they achieved it? He'd already found out the hard way once, the proof is in the data.

The data from less far-flung outposts and observatories was sent to two locations, Haystack Observatory in Westford, Massachusetts, and Bonn, Germany, for processing in their supercomputers. What does that entail? Well, the computers would combine the data, scrub out the useless noise, and match the observations from each observatory down to the second. It took months.

Once the data was correlated, now they needed to understand what the data was *seeing*. They still were missing the data from Antarctica, but looking at what they had, just the numbers, the team was starting to feel confident that they'd gotten something.

Now they wondered, once the full data was in, and if they had gotten that black hole, what would it actually look like in real life? A ring? A disorganized mess? A blur? No one knew for sure. Obviously, there were decades of theories about what leading physicists thought a black hole should look like, but they wanted to see what the telescopes saw.

Meet the Team!
Part 2

Observation nights and tests meant long hours. Those hours could be extremely busy and then pretty dead. EHT members found creative ways to pass the time.

Jupiter and the full Moon from the platform above the SMT dish.
(Credit: Junhan Kim)

And one of them was to hold a photography contest. They each tried to get the most breathtaking shots of their observatories. And the team in Arizona not only managed to capture their telescope, but the planet Jupiter and the Moon as well!

One of the people participating in Arizona operations was PhD student and astronomer Sara Issaoun. She first picked up a telescope at eight years old and was blown away by the possibility of observing planets with her own eyes.

Her family had moved to the Netherlands when she was only fourteen, but Sara had decided to return to Canada for college. In 2014, she planned to spend her summer break in the Netherlands, and hoped to volunteer with research while she was there.

So, she sent Heino an email offering to help with astronomy work. After looking at her resume, Heino brought her on to the EHT project and so began Sara's astronomy career! She would complete her master's and PhD while working on the EHT imaging team. She worked on the data calibration, a critical part of coming up with the image.

Part of the SMT Team. Left to right: Sara Issaoun (Radboud University), Freek Roelofs (Radboud University), Junhan Kim (University of Arizona), Christian Holmstedt (University of Arizona). (Credit: Junhan Kim)

11

NOW WHAT?

Finally, the long Antarctic winter came to an end. That meant it was safe enough for the racks of the South Pole's observation data to be shipped.

On December 13, 2017, a long journey across the world via boat, plane, and trucks came to an end at Haystack Observatory. Now the last bit of more than a half ton of data could be processed.

By now, there were fifty scientists dedicated to just the imaging alone. They divided into four teams. Two teams would process the data at the Max Planck Institute for Radio Astronomy in Bonn, Germany, and two teams would process the data in the United States at Haystack, outside Boston. Katie's team was at Haystack, where Shep was also working. For the two teams in Germany, Heino was

An Event Horizon Telescope imaging team at the Harvard Black Hole Institute on the first day of trying to recover an image of M87's black hole. From left to right: Lindy Blackburn, Katie Bouman, Andrew Chael, Michael Johnson, Lia Medeiros, Maciek Wielgus, Sheperd Doeleman. (Photo courtesy of Katie Bouman)

on hand. They added members to each team from across the collaboration. It was truly a global effort with one important rule.

None of the teams could communicate with one another. No checking in. No updates. Nothing. They also used different methods to translate the data into an image. The point was to see if they all came up with the same image, making sure that the data was dictating the picture, not the human beings.

Heino Falcke checked on his students as they began to process the data. And he knew right then that they had something. It was the math that clued him in, long before they had an image.

"This is like, you don't hear the music, but you see the notes.

You read it but you don't hear the music. You just see the notes written down. And not all of them. Just a fraction of them. But this was enough. You are trained as a scientist. Just like the musician can listen to music when they see it written down, as a scientist you already see this is going to be a very interesting tune. It was exactly the tune we were looking for."[38]

It took seven long, intensely focused weeks of analysis. But at the end of it, all four teams had an image.

When Heino saw the telltale ring for the first time in Germany, now he was hearing the music. "I was hovering over the ground for an hour or so. It was like, 'I know you,'" he explained. "It's like having someone you have fallen in love with, but you have only written letters to. And you have this picture in your mind of what he or she looks like . . . how beautiful. And now you actually see them for the first time face-to-face. You see the real image. And it's exactly the way you pictured it all this time. Wow! It's real."[39]

An hour later, nerve and doubt hit him like a freight train.

"Now you see each other eye to eye, face-to-face. Will that relation hold. Is it true what you are seeing?"[40]

At Haystack, a similar scene played out. Katie was working with her team, Shep next to her. They ran the numbers, and there it was—a ring.

"Whoa!" Shep blurted out as Katie laughed in awe. They couldn't contain their excitement.

"If this holds up," Shep said, "it will be the discovery of my lifetime."[41]

For Katie, this step was amazing. "There's like a ring that started appearing and you're, like, oh my God, we're looking at a black hole. Like you kind of had to pinch yourself every once in a while."[42]

Just like Heino, at first there was the thrill. And then the doubts followed. *Was it real?* They had to be absolutely certain.

"You always have to be careful that you don't fool yourself and see what you want to see . . . That's the most dangerous thing in science, that you so urgently want to see that ring, that you interpret that into your data,"[43] Heino explained.

There was one sure way to find out. Katie would reveal all four pictures from all four teams at once to the group. Only then would they see if they had come up with the same results or not. Like everyone else, she would be seeing them for the first time. Had they really, truly, actually taken a picture of a black hole?

Meet the Team!
Part 3

MICHAEL JOHNSON is an astrophysicist at the Center for Astrophysics at Harvard and the Smithsonian. He also lectures at Harvard. Johnson's focus is on black holes and neutron stars. As part of the EHT, he co-led the imaging teams, working to develop the algorithms and software capable of processing the data and producing an image. When he's not at work, he likes to bring his love of astronomy to students. This work has centered on reaching out to under-represented students and families.

ANDREW CHAEL is an astrophysicist and an Einstein Fellow at the Princeton University Center for Theoretical Science. He was a part of the imaging team. Andrew uses supercomputers to simulate how that bright plasma falls into black holes. He also investigates black hole jets. While studying at Harvard, Michael Johnson, Ramesh Narayan, and Shep were his advisers! He shares some of his computer simulations on his website and also compares a simulation of M87* to the real photo! Andrew is a proud member of the Astronomy and Astrophysics Outlist of LGBTQIA+ members. The entire list is published online.

BOOKSHELF: Andrew Chael worked on coming up with new techniques for processing the data. One of his favorite books? *Contact* (also a major motion picture) by Carl Sagan. Published in 1985, for Andrew, the book captured what was so inspiring about the field. He also loved *2001: A Space Odyssey* by Arthur C. Clarke. In this sci-fi classic, readers follow multi-planetary astronauts on a hunt for evidence of extraterrestrial life. The first time Andrew encountered a black hole was in the pages of this book!

KAZU AKIYAMA is an astrophysicist at Haystack Observatory. He co-led the EHT imaging team with Michael Johnson. Akiyama's area of interests are black holes and space-time. Born, raised, and educated in Japan, he moved to Massachusetts in 2015 to work at Haystack, but has been a part of the EHT since 2010. How did he feel when images were revealed? "It was a remarkable moment,"[44] he said, beaming during a television interview.

LINDY BLACKBURN is a radio astronomer for the Harvard-Smithsonian Center for Astrophysics. As a member of EHT, he led the effort to calibrate all of that raw data. Lindy's scientific investigations focus on black holes and experimental general relativity.

RURIK PRIMIANI was born in Venezuela and studied both engineering and astronomy. His contribution to the Event Horizon Telescope project was developing the digital back end for the telescope to record what the telescopes were picking up.

CHAPTER 12

12

WAIT FOR IT.
WAIT FOR IT . . .

JULY 24, 2018,
CAMBRIDGE, MASSACHUSETTS

Filling the desks of a basement classroom in Cambridge, Massachusetts, the Event Horizon Telescope team knew the moment had come. Katie Bouman stood in front of the room. Shep sat in the front row.

Four teams had independently run the data. They had taught the computers how to see an image from the data. But it's easy to insert your own bias into anything.

So, the four groups had worked for seven weeks in total isolation. Each group agreed not to communicate with any of the other three groups. An extreme measure to avoid bias of any kind. They needed results that could be trusted.

After all of that data crunching, the isolation, the checking and double checking. Had they independently come up with the same image from the same data? Because if all four teams arrived at the same picture . . . then, plain and simple, they had the world's first picture of a black hole. A scientific breakthrough of unimaginable proportions and a jumping-off point for more research, more discovery.

Katie was nervous. Would the images be the same? Would these pictures provide the indisputable seeing-is-believing proof of what black holes actually look like? More teams joined the room via video conference. All eyes were on her.

"I wrote this tool that allowed us to compare our results in a blind way,"[45] she said.

She hadn't even seen the results herself. They were on her computer. She just had to open the file. And once she did, the results would either be scientific breakthrough or . . . back to the drawing board. The stakes were high. The pressure was on.

And up there in front of the world's leading black hole scientists, standing in front of people who had put in endless hours, weeks away from their families, withstood horrific weather, whose careers were riding on these results, all she could think was, "I don't want to do it. I don't want to do it."[46]

Thirty seconds passed as Katie prepared to reveal the four images. And then . . . She did it.

All four pictures had the same diameter. All four images featured a bright ring. All four images showed that ring was significantly brighter at the bottom. The pictures were almost identical. They were staring at a black hole.

The room erupted in applause and laughter. Awe and relief.

Katie Bouman revealing the M87 images for the first time to the collaboration. (Photo courtesy of Katie Bouman)

"They were so afraid they would be different images. But they all looked about the same. It was miraculous and it was a very tough thing to do,"[47] said National Science Foundation Director Dr. France Córdova.

For Katie, she knew there was still work to do, verifying, perfecting all of it, but also there was this: "I mean, it was just like, oh my God, we, we actually have an image, you know?"[48] Yes, they had an image.

BOOKSHELF: Jessica Dempsey was part of EHT as the deputy director of the East Asian Observatory in Hawaii. When she saw the picture for the first time, it had a familiar feel. The image reminded her of the Eye of Sauron from *Lord of the Rings*, a fantasy trilogy by J.R.R. Tolkien. This "Great Eye" featured a black slit of pupil surrounded by a flaming ring of orange and red, just like the real pic of a real black hole!

Meet the Team!
Part 4

As we have seen, it took many scientists and researchers from all over the world, working together to make this dream a reality, and all of them deserve to share the spotlight!

Kazunori Akiyama	Lindy Blackburn
Antxon Alberdi	Jay M. Blanchard
Walter Alef	Ray Blundell
Juan-Carlos Algaba	Wilfred Boland
Alexander Allardi	Katherine L. Bouman
Rodrigo Amestica	Geoffrey C. Bower
Jadyn Anczarski	Michael Bremer
Keiichi Asada	Christiaan D. Brinkerink
Rebecca Azulay	Roger Brissenden
Uwe Bach	Silke Britzen
Anne-Kathrin Baczko	Avery E. Broderick
Frederick K. Baganoff	Dominique Broguiere
David Ball	Thomas Bronzwaer
Mislav Baloković	Sandra Bustamente
John Barrett	Do-Young Byun
Christopher Beaudoin	Roger Cappallo
Bradford A. Benson	John E. Carlstrom
Ryan Berthold	Edgar Castillo-Domínguez
Dan Bintley	Andrew Chael

Chi-kwan Chan

Chih-Cheng Chang

Shu-Hao Chang

Song-Chu Chang

Koushik Chatterjee

Shami Chatterjee

Chung-Chen Chen

Ming-Tang Chen

Yongjun Chen

Ryan Chilson

Ilje Cho

Pierre Christian

Tim C. Chuter

John E. Conway

James M. Cordes

Rodrigo Córdova Rosado

Iain M. Coulson

Thomas M. Crawford

Geoffrey B. Crew

Joseph Crowley

Yuzhu Cui

Jordy Davelaar

John David

Mariafelicia De Laurentis

Roger Deane

Jessica Dempsey

Mark Derome

Gregory Desvignes

Jason Dexter

Matthew Dexter

Sheperd S. Doeleman

Sven Dornbusch

Kevin A. Dudevoir

Sergio A. Dzib

Ralph P. Eatough

Andreas Eckart

Chris Eckert

Neal R. Erickson

Wendeline B. Everett

Aaron Faber

Heino Falcke

Joseph R. Farah

Vernon Fath

Vincent L. Fish

Thomas W. Folkers

Ed Fomalont

David C. Forbes

Raquel Fraga-Encinas

William T. Freeman

Robert Freund

Per Friberg

Christian M. Fromm

David M. Gale

Peter Galison

Charles F. Gammie	Ronald Hesper
Feng Gao	Stefan Heyminck
Roberto García	Akihiko Hirota
Gerlie Geertsema	Luis C. Ho
Olivier Gentaz	Paul Ho
Boris Georgiev	James Hoge
Ciriaco Goddi	Mareki Honma
Roman Gold	Chih-Wei L. Huang
José L. Gómez	Lei Huang
Arturo I. Gómez-Ruiz	Yau-De Huang
David A. Graham	David H. Hughes
Christopher H. Greer	Shiro Ikeda
Ronald Grosslein	C. M. Violette Impellizzeri
Minfeng Gu	Makoto Inoue
Frédéric Gueth	Sara Issaoun
Mark Gurwell	David J. James
Kazuhiro Hada	Buell T. Jannuzi
Daryl Haggard	Michael Janssen
Nils W. Halverson	Britton Jeter
Chih-Chiang Han	Homin Jiang
Kuo-Chang Han	Wu Jiang
Jinchi Hao	Michael D. Johnson
Yutaka Hasegawa	Svetlana Jorstad
Michael H. Hecht	Taehyun Jung
Jason W. Henning	Atish Kamble
Antonio Hernández-Gómez	Mansour Karami
Rubén Herrero-Illana	Ramesh Karuppusamy

Tomohisa Kawashima	Lupin C.-C. Lin
Garrett K. Keating	Michael Lindqvist
Ryan Keisler	Ching-Tang Liu
Mark Kettenis	Kuan-Yu Liu
Jae-Young Kim	Kuo Liu
Jongsoo Kim	Elisabetta Liuzzo
Junhan Kim	Wen-Ping Lo
Kimihiro Kimura	Andrei P. Lobanov
Motoki Kino	Laurent Loinard
Jun Yi Koay	Colin Lonsdale
Patrick M. Koch	Li-Ming Lu
Yusuke Kono	Ru-Sen Lu
Shoko Koyama	Nicholas R. MacDonald
Carsten Kramer	Jirong Mao
Michael Kramer	Sera Markoff
Thomas P. Krichbaum	Daniel P. Marrone
Derek Kubo	Alan P. Marscher
Cheng-Yu Kuo	Ralph G. Marson
John Kuroda	Pierre L. Martin-Cocher
Richard Lacasse	Iván Martí-Vidal
Robert A. Laing	Kyle D. Massingill
Tod R. Lauer	Satoki Matsushita
Sang-Sung Lee	Lynn D. Matthews
Erik M. Leitch	Callie Matulonis
Chao-Te Li	Martin P. McColl
Yan-Rong Li	Stephen R. McWhirter
Zhiyuan Li	Lia Medeiros

Karl M. Menten

Hugo Messias

Zheng Meyer-Zhao

Daniel Michalik

Izumi Mizuno

Yosuke Mizuno

Alfredo Montaña

William Montgomerie

Matias Mora-Klein

James M. Moran

Kotaro Moriyama

Monika Moscibrodzka

Dirk Muders

Cornelia Müller

Andrew Nadolski

Hiroshi Nagai

Neil M. Nagar

Masanori Nakamura

Ramesh Narayan

Gopal Narayanan

Iniyan Natarajan

Santiago Navarro

Joseph Neilsen

Roberto Neri

Chi H. Nguyen

Chunchong Ni

Hiroaki Nishioka

Timothy Norton

Aristeidis Noutsos

Michael A. Nowak

George Nystrom

Hideo Ogawa

Hiroki Okino

Héctor Olivares

Gisela N. Ortiz-León

Peter Oshiro

Tomoaki Oyama

Feryal Özel

Scott N. Paine

Daniel C. M. Palumbo

Harriet Parsons

Nimesh Patel

Ue-Li Pen

Juan Peñalver

Dominic W. Pesce

Neil M. Phillips

Vincent Piétu

Richard Plambeck

Michael Poirier

Aleksandar PopStefanija

Oliver Porth

Nicolas Pradel

Ben Prather

Jorge A. Preciado-López

Rurik A. Primiani	Mahito Sasada
Dimitrios Psaltis	Remi Sassella
Hung-Yi Pu	Tuomas Savolainen
Philippe A. Raffin	Pim Schellart
Alexandra S. Rahlin	F. Peter Schloerb
Venkatessh Ramakrishnan	Karl-Friedrich Schuster
Ramprasad Rao	Lijing Shao
Mark G. Rawlings	Paul Shaw
Alexander W. Raymond	Zhiqiang Shen
George Reiland	Hotaka Shiokawa
Luciano Rezzolla	Kevin M. Silva
Bart Ripperda	Des Small
Christopher Risacher	David R. Smith
Freek Roelofs	William Snow
Alan Rogers	Bong Won Sohn
Eduardo Ros	Jason SooHoo
Mel Rose	Kamal Souccar
Arash Roshanineshat	Don Sousa
Helge Rottmann	T. K. Sridharan
Alan L. Roy	Ranjani Srinivasan
Ignacio Ruiz	William Stahm
Chet Ruszczyk	Anthony A. Stark
Benjamin R. Ryan	Kyle Story
Kazi L. J. Rygl	Fumie Tazaki
Alejandro F. Sáez-Madaín	Paul Tiede
Salvador Sánchez	Remo P. J. Tilanus
David Sánchez-Arguelles	Sjoerd T. Timmer

Michael Titus	George N. Wong
Kenji Toma	David P. Woody
Pablo Torne	Jan G. A. Wouterloot
Tyler Trent	Melvin Wright
Sascha Trippe	Qingwen Wu
Shuichiro Tsuda	Paul Yamaguchi
Ilse van Bemmel	André Young
Huib Jan van Langevelde	Ken Young
Daniel R. van Rossum	Ziri Younsi
Laura Vertatschitsch	Chen-Yu Yu
Jan Wagner	Feng Yuan
Craig Walther	Ye-Fei Yuan
John Wardle	Milagros Zeballos
Ta-Shun Wei	Anton J. Zensus
Jonathan Weintroub	Shuo Zhang
Norbert Wex	Guangyao Zhao
Robert Wharton	Shan-Shan Zhao
Nathan Whitehorn	Ziyan Zhu
Alan R. Whitney	Lucy Ziurys
Maciek Wielgus	

13

SHHH!

Before the world would have its chance to see a black hole, the four images needed to be tested. Again. And again. This time they completely removed human involvement, programming the computer to make objective adjustments based on the data. Then the images were fine-tuned and combined into one trustworthy image of the black hole.

Now they had to keep it a secret. More than 350 scientists, mathematicians, engineers, and support staff all had to keep the secret. They couldn't tell anyone. If the image leaked, if it came out in a way that didn't reflect the unique global collaboration that came together, it could be a disaster and undermine future projects. Every single person involved would have to keep it quiet. Period. It was a massive discovery and they only had one chance to tell the world for the first time.

While parts of the EHT team spent nine months vigorously testing the data, others were trying to answer another huge question: How do you tell the world about such an enormous breakthrough? How do you show the world its first look at a black hole?

Joshua Chamot from the communications and media office for the National Science Foundation had been calling Shep regularly ever since that 2017 observation window to see if they had been successful. Josh would say, "Hey we have got to start planning, because when this breaks it's going to be a big deal."[49] He and his colleagues were anxiously waiting for Shep's green light.

Looking back, Josh felt bad about the constant nagging. But finally, in the fall of 2017, Josh's phone rang. Shep told him to start planning. At that point, they were still processing the data. But he was sure enough for the planning to begin.

Josh rolled up his sleeves and got to work. This was the exciting part for the communications team. Only *part* of the job involves dealing directly with the media. Long before they send out any news alerts, they spend a lot of time thinking about how to talk about something so big, so technical, so important. They have to find the right words to describe what the discovery is, why it's important, and how it was made. Once they figure out exactly how to talk about it, then they start planning the event itself, like who should speak, how, when, where, all of it.

And making this discovery had been a global collaboration. Deciding how to share this news with the rest of the planet also had to be a global collaboration. No matter language differences, no matter cultural differences, they had to work together and agree together how to move forward.

And as Heino points out, in their group of researchers and scientists and in all the institutions backing them, there were "very different ways of talking, very different ways of signaling what you mean. Also, inside a collaboration you have political competition, who has the brightest ideas and so forth? It's actually very hard work to make it work,"[50] he said. Choreographing any announcement would need to take all of that into account.

Dr. Peter Kurczynski from the National Science Foundation was part of the team tackling that. "One of the most basic challenges is when you have people literally all over the world, what time are you going to have a meeting? It's going to be in the middle of the night for somebody because the Earth is round!"

And once they were in these meetings, Peter had to develop ways of getting around cultural differences, political differences, and even personality differences. This could not be a case of the loudest person in the room running the show. After all, in some cultures it's considered rude to speak up to anyone you think has a higher position. In other cultures, it's considered rude not to actively participate. This process wasn't easy.

"Some people may be more introverted and less likely to speak up in a meeting and really express themselves," Peter said. "Whereas other people will be more forceful."[51]

Peter had to build an accepting environment where everyone was valued and could trust that they were going to be heard, respected, and taken seriously.

"Listening is an important skill and not one we can just take for granted," he said.

In meetings, he would pay attention to who was talking and who wasn't talking. Then he would look at those who had been silent and ask, "So how do you feel about what's being said? Do you have an opinion?" Then as a decision was coming together, he would check with everyone in the group, even those who had not said a word. "Is everyone happy with this decision? Is anyone unhappy with this decision?" Peter asked.

These were deliberate efforts to bypass cultural differences and make sure that everyone was involved in the decisions and the process every step of the way.

Now they had to deal with another pressure: The world's science media had a feeling something was going on. Journalists had been following the Event Horizon Telescope project. They'd written about some of the successes along the way, the process, the goals, and covered new funding announcements. They were naturally asking how things were going. Had the team imaged a black hole yet? By now the NSF had poured in more than $20 million, more than any other individual institution. It was natural for America-based reporters to ask if those dollars had been well spent. Success or failure? What was the latest?

The pressure was on to give reporters answers. And yet, the team was committed to not leaking a word of it.

"It took a lot of careful negotiating, building relationships, and being sensitive to other people's needs and concerns in order to keep that loose collaboration together, especially under the time pressures and the pressure everybody felt as the media wanted to know what is the story going to be,"[52] Peter explained.

Still, it's like having a major itch that you can *not* scratch under any circumstances. So the team in China developed a hand sign in the shape of a black hole. Posing for photographs while making this gesture helped them acknowledge the excitement, the thrill, without spilling the beans.

"It's not in a scientist's nature or training to want to keep a secret," Peter explained. "The whole nature of science is that you want to tell people about your discovery."

So they discussed it over and over so that team members could decide for themselves without directly being told not to reveal the discovery. What were the benefits of telling the world together? The benefit was getting the world's attention, showing that the limits of human knowledge had been extended, and inspiring the world with the nature of a global collaboration.

These discussions happened across the team. The media officers and communications team talked to the scientific leaders about it, and in turn the scientists discussed it with their teams. It did not matter how high up you were in the collaboration, everyone had a choice of whether to agree to tell the story this way. And time and time again, everyone arrived at the same conclusion . . . we discovered this together, we will tell the world together.

The Event Horizon Telescope Collaboration Meeting, Nijmegen, November 2018.
(Photo courtesy of Heino Falcke; Credit: D. van Aalst)

The NSF took the lead role in communications, but was careful to make space for the discussions, to create a structure and time line for decision making without pressuring other media officers from other institutions and countries. They would meticulously coordinate with the entire team.

The first decision was to tell the world by hosting a press conference as opposed to a steady drip of smaller stories. This was big, and the announcement should feel big, too.

"You can present the whole story, the complete story, and the factually correct story. Rather than having it come out in a series of half-truths or misperceptions,"[53] Peter said.

Next they decided to have it around the world at the *same* time.

"It's good to share it globally in their language and culture, every country, you have your ambassador talk about the same thing," Heino explained. "The language of science is global, the scientific principles are the same. The human language to talk about it is different, but the underlying principles are the same,"[54] he said.

For Joshua Chamot at the NSF, in the earliest days of planning the announcement, he knew what it would mean to the world. "There was so much going on in the world,"[55] he explained. "To have something that was this pure discovery that was just an opportunity to step back and say the universe is a really interesting place and to think philosophically about what it all means . . . we wanted that."

To achieve that, the communications team decided to make the image of the black hole the centerpiece of these press conferences. They could plan around that. How respect at a public event is shown in the United States is different than in Japan or in Europe or other parts of the world. There are different business customs, different styles in planning and delivering press conferences. Even so, together they scripted the simultaneous press conferences down to the second, reflecting each culture's preference. The image of the black hole would be revealed at exactly the same second.

At NSF headquarters, Dr. Denise Zannino Childree looked at her whiteboard. By now, it was full of color-coded lists. Her job was to pull together all of the details: drafting social media posts, coordinating press conference locations and logistics, getting the panelists together, assembling media packets, translating press releases into more than two dozen languages, and more. She had to be certain that everyone involved stayed focused on the heart and soul of the discovery: the wonder of seeing a black hole.[56]

The week leading up to the press conference was brutal. Everyone involved was under enormous pressure. The media had caught wind of a major development. They were at the door, looking for leaks, scraps, any hint at what EHT had seen, if the project was a success or not.

And somehow, with more than three hundred and fifty scientists and team members involved . . . despite all of them being under pressure, there were no leaks. Not one. Even if there had been bumps along the way, there was still an intense culture of respect. No one betrayed it.

Mission:
To Boldly Go . . .

Something cool was happening as scientists from around the world came together to image a black hole. Dr. Córdova spotted it a mile away and hoped it could inspire future scientists like you.

"What would I say to young people who are inspired by the black hole pic? I would encourage them," she explained. It wasn't just the questions the team was asking, but who was asking them.

"I think that this group of people who did the EHT experiment, they are very different in age and diversity." They came from around the world, some from science, some from math, some from communications, and so

on. Each person brought a different set of talents to the table. And they decided to work together, to work through conflict, to work toward a common goal.

Dr. Córdova was impressed. And impressing her is no small accomplishment.

Dr. France A. Córdova. (Credit: NSF/Stephen Voss)

After all, she not only worked at NASA, she knew Moon walker Neil Armstrong personally, and was running one of the largest and most important scientific research organizations in the world.

"And I commend them for coming together so brilliantly to do something that is very tricky and being committed to the ideal of what it is they wanted to do. And they had a lot of dark nights, which are not the same kind of nights full of stars—just a lot of hard obstacles to overcome."

But they overcame them. And for her, that's the takeaway. You can take on hard science, welcome different perspectives and ways of tackling these problems, and overcome them together for the sake of science and understanding our cosmos and humans' place in that.

"To me, it's the biggest thing you can go after because it really brings us to our own roots, the roots of humanity, the roots of everything that is out there," she said. The roots of humanity, as in: How did we come to be here? Where did that process start in space? How do black holes fit into that picture? What more can we learn about the Big Bang? All of these questions, and the idea of exploring other planets are really about trying to have a better picture of our existence and the cosmos we exist in.

"And trying to understand it and make sense of it all is what I think is our highest aspiration,"[57] she said.

14

ATTENTION!

Finally, on April 10, 2019, the cues were given. The scientists took their seats on stages in six cities around the world: Brussels, Belgium; Lyngby, Denmark; Santiago, Chile; Taipei, Taiwan; Tokyo, Japan; and Washington, DC.

In Washington, NSF Director Dr. France Córdova walked in front of a sea of scientists, science writers, and journalists, all crowded in to learn if the world was finally going to see a black hole. She was about to have the attention of space fans across America, something she could have only dreamed for herself as a little girl.

Growing up in Los Angeles in the 1950s, she looked out of her childhood bedroom window and watched searchlights bounce off the clouds of her neighborhood. Supermarkets used the swirling spotlights to get shoppers' attention and boost sales. But the beaming lights had a different effect on France, focusing her attention on the sky. What was up there? How did it work? What was there to discover? At first, she thought this tendency to ask questions meant a career in journalism. But once she started her job gathering facts for a newspaper, she realized the questions could never go deep enough and that reporting on topics like entertainment just didn't excite her.

"So I just assessed where I was going," she explained. She asked herself where she wanted to be at age thirty. The answer? An astrophysicist. "And I just went after that."[58]

That decision led to a lifelong love of science and astrophysics. Her career as an astrophysicist took her to great heights at NASA and then as director of the National Science Foundation (NSF).

And that's why she knew, as NSF director, that this was going to be the moment of a lifetime. "There are always lots and lots of people that tell you why you shouldn't do something,"[59] she said. And that's why she loved this job and this moment, because she had said yes to a team with big ideas, who were willing to take the risks and do the work.

As Shep fidgeted with a roll of paper, Dr. France Córdova was called up to make some remarks.

Dr. France Córdova onstage at the Washington, DC, press conference.
(Credit: Joshua Chamot)

"You are on the stage. The first thing is, you want to do no harm. You don't want to fall off your chair!"[60] she said, laughing. Although the National Science Foundation was the primary funding source—over the years they had gone way past those early investments and had now spent more than $20 million—France had not seen the image. And that was on purpose. She wanted to see it when the rest of the world saw it.

"Good morning," she said, adjusting the microphone. "Thank you for joining us for this historic moment." After bringing the audience up to speed and driving home the fact that, no, you have not seen a black hole before, no one has, she introduced Shep to the world. He came up to the podium.

"Black holes are the most mysterious objects in the universe," Shep began. He explained how black holes work, that they exist in the centers of most galaxies. He was preparing the world, preparing human beings for what they were about to see.

And then he said simply, "We are delighted to be able to report to you today that we have seen what we thought was unseeable. We have seen and taken a picture of a black hole.

"Here it is," he said. The room filled with only one sound . . . the shutters on news cameras. Then silence of awe. And then loud applause.

Scientists have obtained the first image of a black hole, using Event Horizon Telescope observations of the center of the galaxy M87. The image shows a bright ring formed as light bends in the intense gravity around a black hole that is 6.5 billion times more massive than the Sun. This long-sought image provides the strongest evidence to date for the existence of supermassive black holes and opens a new window onto the study of black holes, their event horizons, and gravity. (Credit: Event Horizon Telescope Collaboration)

At the same time that the image was revealed at the five other press conferences, it appeared on the screen behind Shep.

In Belgium, Heino also took the podium, carefully hitting the same points with equal enthusiasm and awe.

"This is the first ever image of a black hole," he said. Not only did people clap, they jumped to their feet in a standing ovation.

At the very same second, the image was revealed in Santiago, again to a roar of applause. In Taipei, scientists could not hide their smiles as they carefully explained the science, the magnitude, and then revealed the image. Again, applause.

In Japan, the rumble of something else . . . infectious wonder.

Headlines appeared instantly around the globe.

Screenshot of the Google Doodle on April 10, 2019, taken by Denise Zannino Childree.

"We used the entire world to make that image. We gave it to the world and the world embraced it," Heino said. "That was a very warm feeling to see the strong emotional feeling all over the world."[61]

People cried. All over the world. People cried. Scientists cried. On the stage, staring at the image, France was overcome with emotion.

"It was just—how difficult it was to do it and at the end of it, to produce something that was so visually compelling,"[62] she said.

And all of a sudden, a part of the cosmos that had been hidden to us was revealed. Albert Einstein had been proven right. And now there was a new tool to use to investigate other mysteries in the cosmos as well.

"It was just an amazing day," Shep said. "You know, I think that one of the things that people like about this image or that draws them to it, is not just the scientific impact. It's not just seeing the unknown. Although those are both important things. But one of the things that I think speaks to people is that we did it as a team and that we did reach across borders."[63]

In a matter of days, more than a billion people had seen the image. It was on the front page of almost every newspaper around the world, in every language. Radio, television, podcasts, and teachers around the world talked about what this global team had pulled off. The world, stewing in a daily digest of truly awful news headlines, felt a sense of unparalleled wonder. The emotion of the reaction, seeing what the image meant to the world, took the team by surprise.

On April 11, Shep woke up and walked into the hotel lobby. The image was on the front page of the *New York Times*, the *Washington Post*, and the *Wall Street Journal*. Now he was starting to grasp the magnitude of the world's reaction. The stream of bad news had been replaced with discovery, awe, and joy that people from different countries and different backgrounds came together and worked together to make an enormous scientific breakthrough.

The EHT image featured on the front page of the New York Times, *the* Washington Post, *and the* Wall Street Journal. *(Credit: Peter Kurczynski)*

Shep was awestruck. He realized that they had been so focused on the science and the project itself, in getting it right, that "we had lost sight of the fact that the wonder of what we had done would be shared by all of humanity," he said. "And that took us by surprise."

Not only had these scientists come together, peered some fifty-five million light-years away to see something that had never been seen, not only did they launch an entirely new way of doing astronomy, but they had inspired the world in the process.

"So many things divide us, so many things that accentuate the differences between people. So many issues that caused conflict," Shep said. "And here you saw something that by its very nature brought people together. And it's odd to think, you have to go fifty-five million light-years into a different galaxy to unify people. But that's what we did."[64]

That wasn't lost on Heino either. People would stop in the street, teary-eyed. "It was something that was shared around the world and embraced around the world," he said. "That still makes me much more emotional. We made the world happy."[65]

Beyond Prediction

Katie knew the science community would be excited, but the world?

"You can never predict something like that, right? People were so excited. We had no idea we would get that kind of pop culture response," she said. "I was blown away." The image made its way instantly into memes and even *The Tonight Show*.

And then the internet began to focus on another image. One of Katie.

Katie Bouman
April 10, 2019 · 🌐

Watching in disbelief as the first image I ever made of a black hole was in the process of being reconstructed.

 325   69 Comments 46K Shares

Katie Bouman's April 10, 2019, Facebook post.
(screenshot taken January 11, 2021)

It was a shot of her reaction to seeing that fuzzy blob for the very first time. And suddenly the internet invented a story to go with it . . . she became *the woman behind the black hole image*. Some celebrated her, assuming she wasn't getting the credit she deserved. And other darker corners of the web attacked her—for being a woman. Soon followed false reports and conspiracy theories that she wasn't actually that involved in the project at all. It was weird, made-up, and it spread like wildfire.

Feelings and tweets on both sides went viral.

"I was very confused by it," Katie explained. "Because my message has been this was such a team effort. It wasn't just one person with one message. There were many parts. It wasn't just imaging, it was instrumentation and calibration and theory and model setting and everything. And then, so I was very upset that people were giving me the focus when I was, like, no, there's so many, there's a number of people who really should be deserving credit for this."

Boarding a plane for California, Katie tried to just block it all out. She hadn't slept all night, working hard on a presentation she had to give at Caltech. Her plan seemed solid: 1) Prepare material for global announcement of first image ever of black hole and 2) Write presentation for Caltech (aka an audience of some of the world's smartest people).

"I was planning on just doing the presentation the day after the announcement, not knowing how big this would be,"[66] Katie explained.

But then the image of the black hole went viral. And then Katie herself went viral.

"And I just, I don't think I slept at all that night, and tried to put it together. And I was, like, oh my God, I have this talk tomorrow, you know, in the morning, or I think it was at noon, and I don't have anything. And I'm trying to deal with all this viral-ness that's going on and everything."[67]

Then three o'clock in the morning came like a freight train. She discovered all the trolling. "I was obviously devastated,"[68] she said.

But then something amazing happened. The very people who had been working with her on the imaging, on the project—they reached out to her and offered support. "I'm just so grateful for them," she said.

Her colleague, Dr. Andrew Chael, also defended Katie online.

Andrew Chael
@thisgreyspirit

(1/7) So apparently some (I hope very few) people online are using the fact that I am the primary developer of the eht-imaging software library (github.com/achael/eht-ima...) to launch awful and sexist attacks on my colleague and friend Katie Bouman. Stop.

achael/eht-imaging
Imaging, analysis, and simulation software for radio interferometry - achael/eht-imaging
🔗 github.com

Andrew Chael's April 11, 2019, tweet.
(screenshot taken January 12, 2021)

Katie, too, tried to correct the message, that this was a team effort. She tried to acknowledge how happy she was that the world saw and responded to women participating in huge scientific breakthroughs. And then she did something else. Katie turned off her phone.

"I turned it off for a few days, actually, because at first I just couldn't even keep it charged. I mean, I had so many things coming in. It's not like I have a bad phone. I had an iPhone but it just wouldn't stay charged. And, but then, also, I couldn't be distracted by it," she said.

After all, Caltech was her future employer, and this stage, this audience . . . Many scientists work their entire careers without this kind of prestigious and hard-earned opportunity.

"I couldn't screw it up,"[69] she said.

Disciplined and focused, she wrote her presentation. She landed in California, stood before an audience who crowded into an auditorium, and began by saying, "I know right now in the media there is a lot of stuff going around that I single-handedly led this project. That is as far from the truth as possible." As Katie laughed, so did her audience. She continued, "This is the effort of lots and lots of people for many, many years."[70]

Then she totally nailed the rest of her presentation. And she did it without losing an ounce of her infectious enthusiasm.

SEE FOR YOURSELF! YouTube has video of Katie's post-announcement Caltech presentation!

Andrew Chael and Katie Bouman posing with newspapers featuring the M87 image on the front page. (Credit: Lindy Blackburn)

15

NEXT?

For Heino Falcke, the most boring world he can imagine is one without questions. "Maybe hell to me is a world where every question is answered."[71] He is still driven to explore and discover new things. The Event Horizon Telescope team had achieved the impossible, but for Shep and the others this was not the end. It really only opened up more questions.

A still picture is one thing, but a movie is another. What about making a movie of our own black hole, the one at the center of the Milky Way? Remember, all of the data they collected on Sgr A* is still available for processing and translating into an image, or even multiple images that could be edited into a movie.

"The biggest challenge in imaging Sgr A* is the speed at which it evolves," Katie explained. "Blobs of plasma orbit M87* every couple of days, whereas those around Sgr A* complete an orbit every few minutes."[72]

Will the team discover new breakthroughs in physics? Will Einstein's theory of relativity hold up? Those are the types of secrets a movie could reveal.

The team is already adding telescopes around the world. The more telescopes they add, the more they can fill in our picture for an even sharper resolution. They might show us more detail about black hole jets that are capable of extinguishing stars. Could they explain the relationship between black holes and the galaxies they live in?

And what about space-based telescopes? Could those bring even more answers? "Adding fast-moving spacecraft into our existing VLBI network would be a tremendous challenge, of course. But for me," Katie said, "that is part of the appeal."[73]

Heino says it could produce a razor-sharp image. "In space, you don't have the atmosphere," he said, which means less noise, less interference with the image. "You could see black holes as sharp as you see in the movies, and see details of it we can only imagine right now."[74]

For now, the team has made all the data they've already collected available. Anyone can search it to try to improve the image or mine the data for other discoveries. They have also gone back through all earlier data they collected during the tests they ran as they updated telescopes and network trial runs prior to 2017. Using the algorithms that the imaging team came up with, they have been able to produce additional images of M87* and discovered a wobble when the black hole rotates.

> **BE ON THE LOOKOUT!** You may notice that the lower
> left part of the ring appears much brighter than the rest of
> the accretion disk. That's due to something called the Doppler
> Effect. The superheated plasma of that section is moving toward
> us, which makes it appear brighter. Think of it like this. Say you
> are in a dark tunnel and your two best friends are at the other
> end with identical flashlights, shining them at you. One friend
> doesn't move but keeps shining her light. The other friend starts
> walking toward you. The closer he gets, the bigger and brighter
> their combined light appears. But the flashlight that's moving
> closer is still identical to the other flashlight. It only *appears*
> brighter.

Seeing how a black hole changes over time is like opening up a lab for scientists. They can test the theory of general relativity in new ways and learn about black hole behavior. New observation windows are planned, and what discoveries they'll uncover remain to be seen.

Dr. France Córdova sees endless questions that still need to be answered. "In that center of that doughnut is so much mystery, so much that's unknown," she said. "There is just so much left to discover. And that's our deepest mystery. If you want to be a detective, there's lots of clues there. And it's all about putting together the clues and trying to solve these mysteries. And it is solvable."[75]

What about for Heino Falcke? The boy who long ago stayed awake wondering about infinity?

"That is an interesting realization. It's something that's very fundamental in a way," he said. "That we can point to this black hole, for example. We know exactly where it is. We know exactly the space it encompasses. And we know that space exists," he said. "We cannot explore it, based on current physics, with any technique to get to know what's inside it. And live to tell the story."[76]

The key words there are "based on current physics." Because the truth is that it may seem impossible today. But before April 10, 2019, taking a picture of a black hole was also impossible, and yet it happened!

There are still secrets we cannot see. There are still mysteries to be solved.

As for Shep, he's as intense and focused today as he was at the very beginning of this journey. "One of the things about science that's wonderful is that it's not beholden to the quarterly bottom line. It's not beholden to the next election cycle. It's not beholden to the nightly news. It has a long timescale to it. We play the long game in science. And so, for me personally, I feel a real kinship with Einstein and Schwarzschild from a hundred years ago. I feel that we have a hundred-year handshake going on, and I wish they were here," he said. "So for science, history is really alive in a way that I'm not sure it is for other fields."[77]

Just who will take up the baton for the next hundred-year handshake remains to be seen. But one thing is certain, our fascination with black holes and their cosmic mysteries doesn't seem to be dimming any time soon.

BIBLIOGRAPHY

"2017 Nobel Prize in Physics Awarded to LIGO Founders."
LIGO Caltech. https://www.ligo.caltech.edu/page/
press-release-2017-nobel-prize.

Akiyama, Kazu. "Kazu Akiyama, Astrophysicist at MIT Haystack
Observatory." Kazu Akiyama website. Updated September 28,
2020. Kazuakiyama.github.io/pages/aboutme.html.

"APP: ALMA Phasing Project." MIT Haystack Observatory. https://
www.haystack.mit.edu/astronomy/astronomy-projects/
alma-phasing-project/.

Ash, Arvin, dir. *General Relativity Explained Simply & Visually*. YouTube,
June 20, 2020. https://www.youtube.com/watch?v=tzQC3uYL67U.

Bouman, Katherine L. "How to Take a Picture of a Black Hole."
Filmed November 2016 in Brookline, MA. TED Talk accessed
via YouTube, posted April 28, 2017. https://www.youtube.com/
watch?v=BIvezCVcsYs&list=PL8WvAW9JLJ1KtPSq_lDLj8W_
E4Zw9uj_x.

Bouman, Katherine L. "Imaging a Black Hole with the Event Horizon
Telescope." YouTube, Caltech, April 12, 2019. https://www.
youtube.com/watch?v=UGL_OL3OrCE.

Bouman, Katherine L. "The Inside Story of the First Picture of a
Black Hole." *IEEE Spectrum: Technology, Engineering, and Science
News*. January 30, 2020. https://spectrum.ieee.org/aerospace/
astrophysics/the-inside-story-of-the-first-picture-of-a-black-hole.

Borenstein, Seth. "First Black Hole Picture: Event Horizon
Telescope Project Reveals Historic Image." ABC7 San
Francisco, KGO-TV. April 10, 2019. https://abc7news.com/
black-hole-picture-photo-of/5241612/.

Chael, Andrew (@thisgreyspirit). "(1/7) So apparently some (I hope
very few) people online are using the fact that I am the primary
developer of the eht-imaging software library (https://github.
com/achael/eht-imaging) to launch awful and sexist attacks on my

colleague and friend Katie Bouman. Stop." Twitter, April 12, 2019. https://twitter.com/thisgreyspirit/status/1116518544961830918.

Chael, Andrew. "About Me." Andrew Chael website. achael.github.io/.

Chou, Felicia, and Dewayne Washington. "NASA's Fermi Traces Source of Cosmic Neutrino to Monster Black Hole." NASA. July 12, 2018. https://www.nasa.gov/press-release/nasa-s-fermi-traces-source-of-cosmic-neutrino-to-monster-black-hole.

Cofield, Calla. "The Giant Galaxy Around the Giant Black Hole." Phys. org. April 26, 2019. https://phys.org/news/2019-04-giant-galaxy-black-hole.html.

Cofield, Calla. "Gravitational Waves: Ripples in Spacetime." Space. com. October 15 2017. https://www.space.com/25088-gravitational-waves.html.

Crockett, Christopher. "How VLBI Reveals the Universe in Amazing Detail." *EarthSky*, Astronomy Essentials. July 5, 2012. https://earthsky.org/astronomy-essentials/how-vlbi-reveals-the-universe-in-amazing-detail.

Downs, Dermott, dir. *The Flash*. Season 1, episode 23, "Fast Enough." Aired May 19, 2015, on The CW.

"EHT." Feryal Özel website. https://xtreme.as.arizona.edu/~fozel/index.php/project/eht/.

EHT Collaboration, The, et al. "First M87 Event Horizon Telescope Results. I. The Shadow of the Supermassive Black Hole." *ApJL* 875, no. 1, Publisher's Version (April 2019): 1.

EHT Collaboration, The, et al. "First M87 Event Horizon Telescope Results. II. Array and Instrumentation." *ApJL* 875, no. 1, Publisher's Version (April 2019): 2.

EHT Collaboration, The, et al. "First M87 Event Horizon Telescope Results. III. Data Processing and Calibration." *ApJL* 875, no. 1, Publisher's Version (April 2019): 3.

EHT Collaboration, The, et al. "First M87 Event Horizon Telescope
Results. IV. Imaging the Central Supermassive Black Hole." *ApJL*
875, no. 1, Publisher's Version (April 2019): 4.

EHT Collaboration, The, et al. "First M87 Event Horizon Telescope
Results. V. Physical Origin of the Asymmetric Ring." *ApJL* 875, no.
1, Publisher's Version (April 2019): 5.

EHT Collaboration, The, et al. "First M87 Event Horizon Telescope
Results. VI. The Shadow and Mass of the Central Black Hole." *ApJL*
875, no. 1, Publisher's Version (April 2019): 6.

ESO. "Anatomy of a Black Hole." ESO European Southern Observatory.
https://www.eso.org/public/images/eso1907h/.

Event Horizon Telescope. "Breakthrough Discovery in Astronomy:
First Ever Image of a Black Hole." Filmed April 10, 2019, Brussels,
Belgium, by the European Commission. https://www.youtube.com/
watch?v=Dr20f19czeE.

Fisher, Len. "Are Black Holes Hot or Cold?" Science Focus, *BBC
Science Focus* magazine. https://www.sciencefocus.com/space/
are-black-holes-hot-or-cold/.

"Flash, The." IMDB series page. October 7, 2014. https://www.imdb.
com/title/tt3107288/.

"Flash, The." DC Universe Infinite. https://www.dcuniverse.com/
encyclopedia/flash/.

Fletcher, Seth. "Clear Skies, with a Chance of Black Holes."
Scientific American Blog Network. April 11, 2017.
https://blogs.scientificamerican.com/dark-star-diaries/
clear-skies-with-a-chance-of-black-holes/.

Fletcher, Seth. *Einstein's Shadow: A Black Hole, a Band of Astronomers,
and the Quest to See the Unseeable.* New York: Ecco, 2018.

"Foundation." Radboud University. www.ru.nl/english/about-us/
our-university/history/radboudhistory/.

Fraser, Henry, dir. *Black Hole Hunters*. Aired April 12, 2019, on
Smithsonian Channel. https://www.smithsonianchannel.com/
Shows/Black-Hole-Hunters/0/3470276.

Frazier, Sarah. "Why the Sun Won't Become a Black Hole." NASA. September 26, 2019. https://www.nasa.gov/image-feature/goddard/2019/why-the-sun-wont-become-a-black-hole.

GaBany, R. Jay. "A Singular Place: Once Considered a Mathematical Curiosity, Black Holes Have Taken Center Stage in Cosmology." *Cosmotography.* https://www.cosmotography.com/images/supermassive_blackholes_drive_galaxy_evolution.html.

Genzel, Reinhard. "Autobiography of Reinhard Genzel." The Shaw Prize. September 9, 2008. https://www.shawprize.org/prizes-and-laureates/astronomy/2008/autobiography-of-reinhard-genzel.

Gibney, Elizabeth, and Davide Castelvecchi. "Physicists Who Unravelled Mysteries of Black Holes Win Nobel Prize." *Nature* 586, no. 7829 (October 6, 2020): 347–8. https://doi.org/10.1038/d41586-020-02764-w.

Gibson, Emily K. "Why Are Supercomputers So Important for COVID-19 Research?" National Science Foundation. April 17, 2020. https://beta.nsf.gov/science-matters/why-are-supercomputers-so-important-covid-19-research.

Grant, Andrew. "What It Took to Capture a Black Hole." *Physics Today.* April 11, 2019. https://physicstoday.scitation.org/do/10.1063/PT.6.1.20190411a/full/.

Handcock, Katherine. "Astrophysicist Andrea Ghez Wins 2020 Nobel Prize for Physics for Supermassive Black Hole Discovery." A Mighty Girl. October 7, 2020. https://www.amightygirl.com/blog?p=31750.

"Hard-Disk Delivery, Neglected Diseases, and Saturn's Young Rings." *Nature* 552 (December 20, 2017): 296–7. https://doi.org/10.1038/d41586-017-08676-6.

"Heino Falcke Receives Highest Dutch Scientific Award." ASTRON, Netherlands Institute for Radio Astronomy. June 7, 2011, old.astron.nl/about-astron/press-public/news/heino-falcke-receives-highest-dutch-scientific-award/heino-falcke-rec.

"History." MIT Haystack Observatory. https://www.haystack.mit.edu/
     hay/history.html (site discontinued).

Ho, Anna, dir. *Radio Astronomy in Five Minutes*. YouTube, MIT
     Bloggers, September 1, 2012. https://www.youtube.com/
     watch?v=3EcrrLNIWdE.

Howell, Elizabeth. "The Genius of Albert Einstein: His Life, Theories,
     and Impact on Science." Space.com. August 15, 2019. https://www.
     space.com/15524-albert-einstein.html.

"IceCube Quick Facts." IceCube South Pole Neutrino Observatory,
     University of Wisconsin–Madison with the National Science
     Foundation. https://icecube.wisc.edu/about/facts.

"Important Scientists: Karl Schwarzschild (1873–1916)." The Physics of
     the Universe. https://www.physicsoftheuniverse.com/scientists_
     schwarzschild.html.

Isaacson, Walter. *Einstein: The Life of a Genius*. New York: Collins
     Design, 2009.

Johnson, Michael. "Scintillating Astronomy." Scintillating Astronomy.
     https://www.scintillatingastronomy.com/.

Keneally, Meghan. "The Biggest News Stories of 2014." ABC News.
     December 26, 2014. https://abcnews.go.com/International/
     biggest-news-stories-2014/story?id=27466867.

Kennefick, Daniel. *No Shadow of a Doubt: The 1919 Eclipse That
     Confirmed Einstein's Theory of Relativity*. Princeton, NJ: Princeton
     University Press, 2019.

Koren, Marina. "Seeing a Black Hole Through Stephen Hawking's Eyes."
     The Atlantic. March 14, 2018. https://www.theatlantic.com/science/
     archive/2018/03/stephen-hawking-death-black-hole/555653/.

Kruglinski, Susan, and Oliver Chanarin. "Roger Penrose Says Physics
     Is Wrong, from String Theory to Quantum Mechanics." *Discover*
     magazine. June 19, 2009. https://www.discovermagazine.com/the-
     sciences/discover-interview-roger-penrose-says-physics-is-wrong-
     from-string-theory.

MeTV Staff. "The 12 Coolest, Craziest Contraptions MacGyver Ever Made." MeTV. December 1, 2016. https://www.metv.com/lists/the-12-coolest-craziest-contraptions-macgyver-ever-made.

"Mission and Identity." *Radboud University*, https://www.ru.nl/english/about-us/our-university/mission/.

Morgan, Ben, ed. *Space! The Universe as You've Never Seen It Before*. New York: DK, 2015.

National Science Foundation (@NSF). "Dan Marrone of @UofA says in a few weeks of observing, @ehtelescope project collected approx. 1000 disks, 5 petabytes of data, equivalent to 'all of the selfies that 40k people will take in their lifetime.' #RealBlackHole #ehtblackhole." Twitter photo, April 10, 2019. https://twitter.com/nsf/status/1115967168766709760?lang=en.

National Science Foundation. "National Science Foundation/EHT Press Conference Revealing First Image of Black Hole." YouTube, National Science Foundation, April 10, 2019. https://www.youtube.com/watch?v=lnJi0Jy692w.

"Nobel Prize in Physics 2020, The." NobelPrize.org. October 6, 2020. https://www.nobelprize.org/prizes/physics/2020/summary/.

"NSF's Newest Solar Telescope Produces First Images." National Science Foundation, January 29, 2020. https://www.nsf.gov/news/news_summ.jsp?cntn_id=299908.

NSF Public Affairs. "Body Size of the Extinct Megalodon Shark Is Off the Charts." National Science Foundation. October 14, 2020. https://www.nsf.gov/discoveries/disc_summ.jsp?cntn_id=301426.

O'Neill, Ian. "Black Holes Were Such an Extreme Concept, Even Einstein Had His Doubts." History.com. April 10, 2019. https://www.history.com/news/black-holes-albert-einstein-theory-relativity-space-time.

Overbye, Dennis. "Black Hole Hunters." *New York Times*. June 8, 2015. https://www.nytimes.com/2015/06/09/science/black-hole-event-horizon-telescope.html.

Overbye, Dennis. "Refurbishments Complete, Astronauts Let Go of Hubble." *New York Times*. May 19, 2009. https://www.nytimes.com/2009/05/20/science/space/20hubble.html?_r=1.

Parks, Jake. "The Nature of M87: EHT's Look at a
Supermassive Black Hole." Astronomy.com. April 10,
2019. https://www.astronomy.com/news/2019/04/
the-nature-of-m87-a-look-at-a-supermassive-black-hole.

Penrose, Roger. "'Mind over Matter': Stephen Hawking—Obituary
by Roger Penrose." *Guardian* (US). March 14, 2018. https://www.
theguardian.com/science/2018/mar/14/stephen-hawking-obituary.

Plait, Phil. "Bad Astronomy's Review of the Science of *Star Trek*."
TrekMovie.com. May 9, 2009. https://trekmovie.com/2009/05/09/
bad-astronomys-review-of-the-science-star-trek/.

Roelofs, Freek, and Sara Issaoun. "Black Hole Hunting in Arizona."
Black Hole Cam. May 8, 2017. https://blackholecam.org/
black-hole-hunting-in-arizona-by-freek-roelofs-and-sara-issaoun/.

Sample, Ian. "Neutrino That Struck Antarctica Traced to Galaxy
3.7bn Light Years Away." *Guardian* (US). July 12, 2018. https://
www.theguardian.com/science/2018/jul/12/neutrino-that-struck-
antarctica-traced-to-galaxy-37bn-light-years-away.

Smith, Heather R. "What Is a Black Hole?" NASA. August 21, 2018
https://www.nasa.gov/audience/forstudents/k-4/stories/nasa-
knows/what-is-a-black-hole-k4.html.

Steijaert, Mickey. "The Rising Star of Sara Issaoun." Radboud
University. July 22, 2019. https://www.ru.nl/@1229129/
rising-star-sara-issaoun/.

Stein, James. "The Schwarzschild Radius: Nature's Breaking Point."
NOVA, PBS. December 20, 2011. https://www.pbs.org/wgbh/nova/
article/the-schwarzschild-radius-natures-breaking-point/.

"What Are Radio Telescopes?" National Radio Astronomy Observatory,
National Science Foundation. November 27, 2019. https://public.
nrao.edu/telescopes/radio-telescopes/.

"What Is a Light-Year?" NASA. August 27, 2020. https://spaceplace.
nasa.gov/light-year/en/.

Whitwam, Ryan. "It Took Half a Ton of Hard Drives to Store the Black Hole Image Data." ExtremeTech.com. April 11, 2019. https://www.extremetech.com/extreme/289423-it-took-half-a-ton-of-hard-drives-to-store-eht-black-hole-image-data.

Willumsen, Gail, dir. *The Science of Interstellar*. Los Angeles: Paramount Pictures Corp, and Burbank, CA: Warner Bros. Entertainment, 2014.

Wolpert, Stuart. "UCLA Astronomers Discover Star Racing Around Black Hole at Center of Our Galaxy." UCLA. October 4, 2012. https://newsroom.ucla.edu/releases/ucla-astronomers-discover-star-239172.

Zuidweg, Martine, and Stan van Pelt. "Team Led by Heino Falcke Presents the First Photograph of a Black Hole." *Vox*, independent magazine of Radboud University. April 10, 2019. https://www.voxweb.nl/international/team-led-by-heino-falcke-presents-the-first-photograph-of-a-black-hole.

ENDNOTES

1 Author interview with EHT Director Dr. Sheperd Doeleman. October 25, 2019.

2 Author interview with EHT Director Dr. Sheperd Doeleman. October 25, 2019.

3 Author interview with EHT Director Dr. Sheperd Doeleman. October 25, 2019.

4 Author interview with EHT Director Dr. Sheperd Doeleman. October 25, 2019.

5 Author interview with EHT Director Dr. Sheperd Doeleman. October 25, 2019.

6 Author interview with EHT Director Dr. Sheperd Doeleman. October 25, 2019.

7 Author interview with EHT Director Dr. Sheperd Doeleman. October 25, 2019.

8 Author interview with EHT Director Dr. Sheperd Doeleman. October 25, 2019.

9 Author interview with EHT Director Dr. Sheperd Doeleman. October 25, 2019.

10 Author interview with EHT Director Dr. Sheperd Doeleman. October 25, 2019.

11 "The Nobel Prize in Physics 2020, The." NobelPrize.org.

12 Fraser, Henry, dir. *Black Hole Hunters*. Time code 4:59.

13 Fraser, Henry, dir. *Black Hole Hunters*. Time code 6:17.

14 Author interview with EHT Director Dr. Sheperd Doeleman. October 25, 2019.

15 Author interview with EHT Director Dr. Sheperd Doeleman. October 25, 2019.

16 "Mission and Identity." *Radboud University.*

17 Author interview with EHT's Dr. Heino Falcke. September 16, 2019.

18 Author interview with EHT's Dr. Heino Falcke. September 16, 2019.

19 Author interview with EHT's Dr. Heino Falcke. September 16, 2019.

20 Author interview with EHT Director Dr. Sheperd Doeleman. October 25, 2019.

21 Author interview with EHT's Dr. Heino Falcke. September 16, 2019.

22 Author interview with NSF Director Dr. France Córdova. August 14, 2019.

23 Author interview with NSF Director Dr. France Córdova. August 14, 2019.

24 Fraser, Henry, dir. *Black Hole Hunters*.

25 Author interview with EHT's Dr. Katherine L. Bouman. November 25, 2019.

26 Author interview with EHT's Dr. Katherine L. Bouman. November 25, 2019.

27 Author interview with EHT's Dr. Katherine L. Bouman. November 25, 2019.

28 Author interview with EHT's Dr. Katherine L. Bouman. November 25, 2019.

29 Author interview with EHT's Dr. Katherine L. Bouman. November 25, 2019.

30 Author interview with EHT's Dr. Katherine L. Bouman. November 25, 2019.

31 Author interview with EHT's Dr. Katherine L. Bouman. November 25, 2019.

32 Author interview with EHT's Dr. Katherine L. Bouman. November 25, 2019.

33 Fletcher, Seth. *Einstein's Shadow: A Black Hole, a Band of Astronomers, and the Quest to See the Unseeable*.

34 Author interview with EHT's Dr. Heino Falcke. September 16, 2019.

35 National Science Foundation (@NSF). Twitter photo, April 10, 2019.

36 Event Horizon Telescope. "Breakthrough Discovery in Astronomy: First Ever Image of a Black Hole."

37 Author interview with EHT Director Dr. Sheperd Doeleman. October 25, 2019.

38 Author interview with EHT's Dr. Heino Falcke. September 16, 2019.

39 Author interview with EHT's Dr. Heino Falcke. September 16, 2019.

40 Author interview with EHT's Dr. Heino Falcke. September 16, 2019.

41 Fraser, Henry, dir. *Black Hole Hunters*.

42 Author interview with EHT's Dr. Katherine L. Bouman. November 25, 2019.

43 Author interview with EHT's Dr. Heino Falcke. September 16, 2019.

44 Andrew, Grant. "What it Took to Capture a Black Hole."

45 Author interview with EHT's Dr. Katherine L. Bouman. November 25, 2019.

46 Author interview with EHT's Dr. Katherine L. Bouman. November 25, 2019.

47 Author interview with NSF Director Dr. France Córdova. August 14, 2019.

48 Author interview with EHT's Dr. Katherine L. Bouman. November 25, 2019.

49 Author interview with NSF's Josh Chamot. September 20, 2019.

50 Author interview with EHT's Dr. Heino Falcke. September 16, 2019.

51 Author interview with NSF Program Director of Astronomical Sciences Dr. Peter Kurczynski. September 20, 2019.

52 Author interview with NSF Program Director of Astronomical Sciences Dr. Peter Kurczynski. September 20, 2019.

53 Author interview with NSF Program Director of Astronomical Sciences Dr. Peter Kurczynski. September 20, 2019.

54 Author interview with EHT's Dr. Heino Falcke. September 16, 2019.

55 Author interview with NSF's Josh Chamot. September 20, 2019.

56 Author interview with NSF's Dr. Denise Zannino Childree. April 8, 2021.

57 Author interview with NSF Director Dr. France Córdova. August 14, 2019.

58 Author interview with EHT Director Dr. Sheperd Doeleman. October 25, 2019.

59 Author interview with EHT Director Dr. Sheperd Doeleman. October 25, 2019.

60 Author interview with NSF Director Dr. France Córdova. August 14, 2019.

61 Author interview with EHT's Dr. Heino Falcke. September 16, 2019.

62 Author interview with NSF Director Dr. France Córdova. August 14, 2019.

63 Author interview with EHT Director Dr. Sheperd Doeleman. October 25, 2019.

64 Author interview with EHT Director Dr. Sheperd Doeleman. October 25, 2019.

65 Author interview with EHT's Dr. Heino Falcke. September 16, 2019.

66 Author interview with EHT's Dr. Katherine L. Bouman. November 25, 2019.

67 Author interview with EHT's Dr. Katherine L. Bouman. November 25, 2019.

68 Author interview with EHT's Dr. Katherine L. Bouman. November 25, 2019.

69 Author interview with EHT's Dr. Katherine L. Bouman. November 25, 2019.

70 Bouman, Katherine L. "Imaging a Black Hole with the Event Horizon Telescope."

71 Author interview with EHT's Dr. Heino Falcke. September 16, 2019.

72 Bouman, Katherine L. "The Inside Story of the First Picture of a Black Hole."

73 Bouman, Katherine L. "The Inside Story of the First Picture of a Black Hole."

74 Author interview with EHT's Dr. Heino Falcke. September 16, 2019.

75 Author interview with NSF Director Dr. France Córdova. August 14, 2019.

76 Author interview with EHT's Dr. Heino Falcke. September 16, 2019.

77 Author interview with EHT Director Dr. Sheperd Doeleman. October 25, 2019.

ACKNOWLEDGMENTS

On April 10, 2019, like many of the world's other space fans, I was sitting at my computer, waiting. Sipping coffee from my beloved Star Trek mug, I wanted to discover if human beings had pulled off the impossible. Had they taken the first ever image of a black hole? At Shep's cue, there it was. A black hole. I found myself teary-eyed over the enormous breakthrough, over what human beings could accomplish, and what we learned about our cosmos.

Right then and there, I wanted to write about this incredible quest to see the un-seeable. Getting to know many of the scientists and team members, to hear firsthand about their dreams, the obstacles they overcame, and what this experience meant to them, has been the experience of a lifetime. Thank you.

When I first reached out to the National Science Foundation, they jumped at the chance to bring this amazing breakthrough to young readers, to inspire future scientists and science communicators. This book would not have been possible without their enthusiastic help and access. My heartfelt thanks to the National Science Foundation, especially Joshua Chamot, former director Dr. France Córdova, Dr. Denise Zannino Childree, and Dr. Peter L. Kurczynski. I am so grateful for the time and help of EHT group members, particularly Dr. Sheperd Doeleman, Dr. Katie Bouman, Dr. Heino Falcke, Dr. Andrew Chael, and Dr. Harriet Parsons. To the entire team, thank you for everything you did to show us more of our cosmic home.

To Holly West, my incredible editor, your support has been

unbelievable. This project came together at a personally difficult moment for me, the death of my mother. Your steady hand, sharp editorial instincts, encouragement, and patience made all the difference. I am truly appreciative. Thank you to Raphael Geroni, who designed this book and whose work never fails to impress. Thank you to Jean Feiwel and the entire team at Feiwel & Friends and Macmillan.

To my agent, Ammi-Joan Paquette, thank you for your guidance, support, cheering, and friendship. It is an honor and a treat to make this journey with you and everyone at the Erin Murphy Literary Agency. Thank you to my writing critique group: Laurie Warchol, Darlene Ivy, Rachel Davis, Helen Stevens, and Melanie Ellsworth.

To my friends and family, thank you for your joy and support on the tough days. To my fellow space fan and big brother, Patrick Crowley, thank you for your love and friendship (and idea for the title of this book!)

Last but not least, to my partner, Liam McCoy, loving you is the gift of a lifetime. I am so lucky. And to our five kids (in order of youngest to oldest), Quinn, Crowley, Brady, William, and Sally, may the starry night sky always remind you of all that is possible.